HISTORIC BALDWIN COUNTY
A Bicentennial History

by Dr. Larry Burnette

Commissioned by the Alabama Gulf Coast Area Chamber of Commerce and
the Eastern Shore Chamber of Commerce

Historical Publishing Network
A division of Lammert Incorporated
San Antonio, Texas

CONTENTS

First Edition

Copyright © 2007 Historical Publishing Network

All rights reserved. No part of this book may be reproduced in any form or by any means, electronic or mechanical, including photocopying,

without permission in writing from the publisher. All inquiries should be addressed to

Historical Publishing Network, 11555 Galm Road, Suite 100, San Antonio, Texas, 78254. Phone (800) 749-0464.

Alabama Gulf Coast Area Chamber of Commerce and Eastern Shore Chamber of Commerce are not responsible for historical accuracy.

ISBN: 978-1-893619-80-7

Library of Congress Card Catalog Number: 2007943858

Historic Baldwin County: An Illustrated History

author: O. Lawrence Burnette, Jr.

cover artist: Blarche Sumrall

contributing writers for "Sharing the Heritage":   Marie Beth Jones, Eric Dabney, Scott Williams

Historical Publishing Network

president: Ron Lammert

project manager: Lou Ann Murphy

director of operations: Charles A. Newton, III

administration: Donna M. Mata, Melissa Quinn, Evelyn Hart

book sales: Dee Steidle

production: Craig Mitchell, Colin Hart

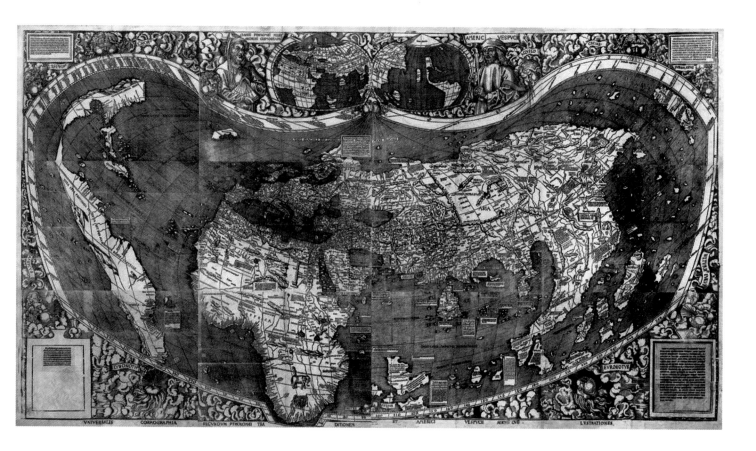

CHAPTER I

IN THE BEGINNING...

In the beginning there was a remarkable and lovely strand of coastline on the Gulf of Mexico, marked by emerald-green water and sugar-white sand beaches, covered with tall pines and stately live-oaks, and stretching between two bays which came to be known as Mobile and Perdido. That area came to be Baldwin County in the State of Alabama, and this is the story of it's colorful and important history, a history whose lengthened shadow is larger than itself.

Even so, Baldwin is huge. Roughly rectangular, measuring about 40 miles east to west and 80 miles south to north, it is bounded by water on the east, south, and west, contains some 22,500 acres—the largest in Alabama and one of the largest in the United States. Until about 1900 it remained one of the most remote and isolated areas in the United States, difficult to reach except by water, yet blessed with an abundance of resources. It is a land which the normal process of development overlooked, a throwback to the frontier of earlier years long after it had pressed on far into the trans-Mississippi West.

The land in Baldwin contains some of the richest and deepest of sandy-loam soils, as those who found their way to its shores discovered, native Americans as well as the first pioneers. The county is a flat plateau which gradually slopes to the sea, watered by deep rivers draining south, east, and west. In pre-historic times, the eastern and western boundaries were river valleys, which slowly flooded and became bays as the polar ice caps melted at the end of the Ice Age. The one on the west, named "Bahia Espiritu Santo" (Bay of the Holy Spirit) by the Spanish, was later renamed Mobile Bay by the French, and it is the outlet to the sea for the waters from fully half of Alabama. The smaller bay to the east, the current boundary between Florida and Alabama, was named "Bahia Perdido", and in its English form of Perdido (or Lost) Bay, the name stuck.

Martin Waldseemüller's 1507 world map, the first known map to refer to "America."

COURTESY OF THE LIBRARY OF CONGRESS

The climate of the Gulf Coast is hot, wet—and often violent. More than 60 inches of rain falls annually, and the mean temperature is about 60, with highs in the upper 90's and lows in the 40's. Freezing temperatures are rare and last for only a day or two. But the most impressive climatic phenomena are the recurring hurricanes which roar out of the Gulf to strike the coast with a force to shake the faith of newcomers. These storms have been a part of the distinctive forces which have shaped the history of the Gulf Coast.

The first human beings arrived on the Gulf Coast shortly after 10,000 B.C.E., a part of the peopling of the American Continent by Asiatic stock crossing the Bering Strait while it was a land bridge caused by the Ice Age. These first arrivals have left traces of a culture marked by communal male hunting, stone and pottery objects, elementary food gathering by females, and trips to the Gulf shore for an annual summer celebration. Gradually these first native peoples evolved into a higher culture known as the Mississippi Stage, marked by the development of the bow and arrow, the cultivation of staple foodstuffs, long-distance trade, permanent settlements, and a highly structured tribal organization, all of which peaked several centuries before the arrival of the first European explorers, about 1,200 to 1,400 A.D. At that time, the native population of what was to become Baldwin County is estimated to have been approximately 5,000.

By about 1,500 A.D. the various bands and chiefdoms in Alabama had evolved into several recognizable tribes, all using the same Muskhogean language and sharing the same culture of the Creeks and their neighbors, the Choctaw, Chickasaw, Cherokee, and a smaller tribe of Alibamu (the origin of the name of the state). However, a common language and culture was about all they shared, for they continually contested favored hunting grounds and influence. Most of the native inhabitants of Baldwin were Creeks, with frequent intrusion by the Seminoles, who populated the area to the east in what is today northwest Florida. The Creeks were an impressive people, erect and of slender build, with olive complexions, and were somewhat taller than neighboring tribes. Distinctively, they wore their hair plucked except for a central ridge, which bore feathers or shells for ornamentation. Creek women wore their hair in long braids.

There is a charming but unverified legend that a group of Welshmen, led by a Prince Madoc, were the first Europeans to land on the Gulf Coast at Mobile Bay about 1170. Accounts persist of their supposed trek inland as far as present-day Chattanooga, and legend survived among the Cherokee of a band of "white people" who built stone forts and who were ultimately absorbed by the Indians. Physical or documentary evidence of the Welsh colony has not been found, so the legend must be regarded as just that.

The first documented European landings along the Gulf Coast were those of a group of swashbuckling Spanish explorers, who were encouraged by the Spanish crown to search out the land and stake out a claim against the rival interests of England. In these first explorations the Spanish were not totally ignorant, for they had the benefit of a 1507 map of the Gulf Coast drawn by the German mapmaker, Martin Waldsemueller. The source of his information, while remarkably accurate, remains a mystery. Like those in South America, the early Spanish explorers of the Gulf Coast were looking for gold, but they found only pure white sand beaches and magnificent forests, so they continued in their vain searches and left behind only a thin veneer of Spanish culture. Other areas in Central and South America were to be the main attractions for the Spanish until they were pushed aside in the Gulf region by France and England.

While Spanish expansion in that area was not successful, it was not from lack of trying by a remarkable group of conquistadores, who throughly explored the Gulf Coast. First, there was Alonzo Alvarez de Pineda, who in 1519 scouted the coast from Apalachicola to the Mississippi, thereby claiming the honor of being the first European of record to see the area between Perdido and Mobile bays, the future area of Baldwin County. He spent several weeks exploring the area and cultivating the Creeks before concluding that the area was attractive for settlement but unpromising for trade.

Pineda was followed in 1527 by Panfilio de Navarez, who secured from the Spanish crown the title of adelantado (sub-governor) and the right to plant a colony at his own expense. His expedition was extensive, embracing 300 men and a number of vessels, but it floundered due to the fatal errors of hostility and cruelty to the Indians. Navarez split his forces, sending his fleet (with most of his supplies) ahead of his main force, which sloshed along the coast while fending off Indians attacks. Infuriated by his failure to find quick profits in the form of gold, Navarez noted that the Gulf Coast was "difficult to travel and wonderful to look at;" yet the obvious natural resources made little impression on him. Without any tangible, material profits from the enterprise, the Navarez expedition desperately slaughtered its horses for food,

constructed several rough barges as transport across the Gulf, and set off by water for the safety of Mexico. Several years later, the survivors stumbled into a Spanish outpost in western Mexico.

Bereft of the detailed knowledge of those who preceded, Hernando de Soto was nevertheless fairly well informed about the area he was about to explore in 1539. Leaving Spain with a fleet of seven ships and a band of over 500 armed men, he recklessly plunged into the interior of the Gulf coast at the site the future Tampa, needlessly fighting the natives along his entrada for the next four years. The exploration ranged through the interior of Georgia and South Carolina to southeast Tennessee, thence generally southwest across Alabama, then northwest across Mississippi. The precise location of de Soto's route is open to debate because the explorer frequently did not himself know where he was, and the scribes of the

A map of Baldwin County.

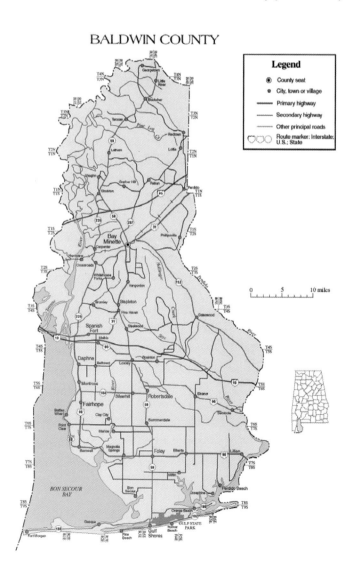

expedition were often more concerned to record their observations of native customs and manners than accurately to describe the areas through which they traveled. The highlight of de Soto's journey was undoubtedly his fateful encounter with Chief Tuscaloosa in central Alabama, which seems to have both sobered the Spanish conquistador and moved him to give up a planned reunion with his wife and his supply train, both having been planned for either Mobile Bay or Pensacola. Instead, de Soto marched across Mississippi to the great river, the Mississippi. There he contracted a fatal fever, and was buried beneath its waters to insure against native reprisals against his remains. The remnants of de Soto's expedition struggled by land and sea to reach the coast of Mexico, and the failure did much to deflate the Spanish expectations of the wealth to be found in the interior of North America.

The next Spanish effort to colonize the Gulf Coast was undertaken in 1558-1559 by the Portugese explorer, Guido de los Bozares, then in the service of Philip II. Bozares first focused attention on Mobile Bay, which he named the Bay of Filipina, being especially impressed by the high ground along the eastern shore of the future Baldwin County. The weight of evidence favors the Bay of Filipina as that of Mobile rather than Pensacola, but there are scholars who are convinced to the contrary. In any event, on the basis of the Bozares expedition, in 1540 a second expedition was led by Captain Diego Moldonado. The permanent features of Mobile Bay which was painstakingly described in such detail make it virtually certain that the Mondolado account was to Mobile and not Pensacola Bay. Soon, a new expedition was sent out from Mexico under the command of the colorful Tristan de Luna. He brought with him a company of 500 soldiers and more than 1,000 settlers, including several women and children, and supplies to last about seven years. His destination was probably Mobile Bay, but another group of Florida historians claim bragging rights for Pensacola primarily on the basis of a recent find of one of de Luna's ships wrecked at the mouth of Bayou Texar by a hurricane in 1559. Whether the locale was Mobile or Pensacola Bay, while unloading the extensive stores, the de Luna expedition was overtaken by a massive hurricane, which provided a fatal blow to the colony. The hurricane which denied the colony that distinction of being the first permanent European settlement in North America eventually led the harried and dejected settlers to relocate to St. Augustine, Florida. Within the silent land which lay between Mobile and Pensacola bays was the site of the abortive first effort of Spain to expand its colonial empire into North America.

The next attempt to colonize the Gulf Coast did not take place until 1630. In that year the Spanish crown awarded a substantial tract on the western shore of Perdido Bay to the Suarez brothers, Jose, Rosa, and Francisco, cattle ranchers who relocated from Cuba. Several generations are buried in the Suarez cemetery at Spanish Cove, just south of Lillian. This marks the first recorded settlement within the current boundaries of Baldwin County, a lonely outpost of European civilization.

Spain continued to make occasional efforts to explore the Gulf Coast, gradually focusing its attention on Pensacola Bay, but the French and English were also eyeing the area as a convenient locale to anchor their own colonial ambitions in the area. After the defeat of the Spanish Armada in 1588, the capacity of Spain's power to contest for control of the Gulf Coast gradually weakened, which was matched by the rise of French power and influence. As de facto allies against England, Spain and France gradually came to recognize Perdido Bay as the boundary between their respective spheres of influence; Pensacola being the seat of Spanish Florida, while Mobile became the capital of New France. With telling irony, the boundary water between the two became the convenient seat of operations for English pirates, who plucked their profit from the Spanish galleons which lumbered along the Gulf shore laden with the spoils of Central and South America. In the grand sweep of history, it was the pirate nation (England and its heirs) which ultimately won the contest for control of the Gulf Coast. The area of Baldwin County became the stage on which a large part of the drama was played out.

Instead of contributing to the material profit of Spain's colonial empire, the Gulf Coast efforts were all total losses. Each year Spain contributed a subsidy, but mismanagement and graft siphoned even the stream of subsidy, so that the relatively few colonists who braved the Gulf settlement were forced to rely on food supplies from the Indians. Because failure seemed endemic, the Spanish were never moved to establish an effective system of civil government. Instead, their Gulf colonies continued to function as permanent military expeditions under the command of military officers. Spanish Indian policy was haphazard, forming a fertile opportunity for corruption. That came to a sudden end with the arrival of French colonial interest in the Gulf area.

Following King William's War, by the Treaty of Ryswick, France and Spain thereafter joined forces in the Gulf region in common purpose to prevent the expansion of English colonial designs. France had previously confined its American interests to Canada, but now it began to push down the Mississippi River to the Gulf, then along its shore to the East. Robert Cavelier, Sieur de la Salle, in 1682 reached the mouth of the Mississippi and claimed the area for France. After la Salle was killed in attempting to establish a colony on the Texas coast, his friend Henri de Tonti, the "Iron Hand," succeeded him as the commanding French presence along the Gulf Coast. The key to his success was his Indian policy, firmness coupled with friendship.

The leadership of the French colonial efforts in the Gulf region ultimately fell into the hands of a remarkably able and experienced military leader, French Canadian Pierre Le Moyne d'Iberville. Together with his younger brother, Jean-Baptiste Le Moyne de Bienville, he sailed from France with a force of about 200 colonists, including women and children, reaching the port of Pensacola in January, 1699. Finding the Spanish already established there, the French expedition sailed further west to Mobile Bay, making a landing at the site of the future Fort Morgan on January 31, 1699. "This land is unwooded sand dunes," d'Iberville wrote in his journal. Four days later the French made the first contact with the native population of the future Baldwin County in the person of an elderly native who was too ill to run away. He was given gifts and tobacco, and the reports of such kindness paved the way for good will for years to come.

After being assured that the Spanish at Pensacola did not pose a threat, d'Iberville explored up the Alabama River which emptied into Mobile Bay and discovered high ground about twenty

miles up stream from the present-day site of Mobile. There he laid out a town to be named Mobile after a band of Creeks called the Mobilients. The vast expanses of virgin forest in Baldwin held little interest for the French; other than a fishing settlement at Bon Secour and several farms east of the Delta area, the future Baldwin County remained unsettled under French control.

D'Iberville died in 1706, leaving his brother, Bienville, to lead the new French colony on the Gulf Coast. Under his command, Mobile was relocated downstream to its present location, guarded by a new fort along the waterfront. The new site proved to be propitious, and the town flourished. From 1711 until 1719 it was the capital of the entire Louisiana Territory, the land of the future Baldwin County being its far eastern frontier, a pleasant refuge of escape from the ravages of heat and fevers during the summer.

The Eastern Shore was used as an area of relaxation by the French in Mobile, hunting and fishing lodges being built there by the Le Moyne brothers. In addition, about 1700 the fishing village of Bon Secour ('the best chapel of ease") was settled. Also on the Eastern Shore in 1715 Joseph Simon de la Pointe received a land grant of one league [about two miles] at the mouth of Weeks Bay, and somewhat later Augustin Rochon established a plantation near Spanish Fort. British naval charts of the 1770's show both settlements.

The French and Indian War changed the map of North America. France was then forced to surrender all its claims to North America; the

Louisiana Territory west of the Mississippi was transferred to Spain, while the Floridas, both East and West, came into the possession of Great Britain. Now for the first time, the area of the future Baldwin County came under English control. Actually, it made little difference for the immediate future. Other than stimulating the issuance of English land grants, what really changed was the growing stream of American squatters who found their way to the vast tracts of virgin land now under nominal control of England.

The English traditions of good order and discipline soon brought an end to the years of neglect which had characterized Spanish and French rule along the Gulf Coast. Britain created two colonies, East and West Florida, the boundaries of the latter being from Apalachicola to the Mississippi and south of the thirty-first parallel. Now the area of Baldwin was ruled from Pensacola instead of Mobile, and it shortly had vast additional lands added when the boundary was pushed north to 32 degrees 28 minutes, the latitude of the former Fort Toulouse. Moreover, by the Proclamation of 1763, the British outlawed American settlement west of the Alleghenies, a move which was designed to protect the Indians but which actually helped push the Americans into rebellion in the Revolution.

The military authority of British West Florida was Major Robert Farmar, who after an initial inspection of the defenses of the area declared them inadequate. At the same time, an informal census counted 350 inhabitants in Mobile and 124 scattered in 17 plantations on the Eastern Shore. The French habitants were required to swear allegiance to Great Britain, or remove themselves forthwith, and many elected the latter alternative. Initially, they relocated to New Orleans but finding things even less to their liking there, they gradually drifted back to their former homes and plantations. Farmar himself became enamored of the opportunities on the Eastern Shore and after retiring from the British Army became a plantation owner at Farm Hall near Stockton. There he hosted the botanist William Bartram while conducting his research on the Gulf Coast.

The first British governor of West Florida was George Johnstone, a career naval officer with political connections, but he turned out to be a complete failure at civil administration. He was at cross purposes with every other officer of the colony, and he championed the Stamp Act, which was as detested in West Florida as in the Eastern seaboard colonies. His only redeeming success was his Indian policy, which resulted in securing the loyalty and co-operation of many of the tribes of the old Southwest, precisely what was most needed to secure the tenuous hold by which Britain held the area. The Johnstone administration ended in 1766 and was succeeded by several others of short term. Meanwhile, Americans poured into the colony, influenced in large measure by the publications of Bartram, the Pennsylvania naturalist. Nominally Loyalist, the political sense of the region gradually turned towards favoring American independence and annexation, only thinly hidden from the British colonial officials.

Without the reliable loyalty of the inhabitants, the British administrators of West Florida cultivated the Indians of the coastal interior as their most dependable allies against the backdrop of rumored and actual uprisings against the crown. One such plot was that led by James Willing, who after instigating a riot in Natchez escaped to northern Baldwin with a copy of the Declaration of Independence. Although Willing was arrested and confined in Mobile until 1779, his agitation resulted in a popular movement demanding the removal of Governor Peter Chester.

Even before the Battle of Yorktown won independence for the American cause, another turn of European politics influenced the future of the Gulf Coast. In 1780 Spain openly joined the war against Britain, thereby hoping again to secure a toe-hold in North America, and she dispatched the young and colorful Bernardo Galvez, Governor of Louisiana, to unseat British control of West Florida by an attack on Mobile. Without much of a fight, the British garrison surrendered to the superior Spanish attack force. The same scenario was repeated the next year at Pensacola.

Thus at about the same time that American independence was being established at Yorktown, British influence was being removed in West Florida. From the American perspective, it was acceptable that Spain be left in temporary and nominal control of the Gulf Coast. She had previously tried and failed to successfully colonize the area, and in weak, non-British hands, it was ripe for plucking when the time was right.

CHAPTER II

IN THE EYE OF AN INTERNATIONAL HURRICANE

By force of arms Spain captured Mobile and Pensacola, but it did not secure legal title until the Treaty of Paris in 1783. By that agreement, Spain regained both East and West Florida, everything east of the Mississippi and south of the thirty-first parallel. Even this arrangement was reached in secret, the result of private machinations between the American and British negotiators plotting against the Spanish. Those understandings reached in secrecy were to flower in a period of international intrigue, filibustering, and Indian diplomacy which engulfed the Mobile-Pensacola area for years until the influence of the Spanish, filibusterers, and Indians was finally removed. Such was the environment in which the future Baldwin County came into being.

Following the end of the Revolution, north of the disputed boundary between the United States and Spanish Florida, natural expansion and land speculation propelled thousands into the area west of the Appalachians as if the Indians who still lived there were of no consequence. In 1785 Georgia organized its frontier, which stretched all the way to the Mississippi, for the benefit of land speculators, who bought large tracts from several Yazoo land companies and who placed increasing pressure on the Indian tribes which stood in their way. South of the boundary with Spanish Florida, a new colonial policy was adopted which aimed at preventing the area from being overrun by Americans by using the Indians, especially the Alabama Creeks, as a buffer. This brought to the fore a remarkable native chief, Alexander McGillivray, who ruled from his plantation at Little Tallahassee, near Fort Toulouse. Until his death in 1793, by extraordinary cunning and guile he protected his people from being ground up in the conflict between Spain and the new American nation, all the while freely crossing the border with Spanish Florida. In the process, he also amassed great wealth and probably helped Spain hold on to its Florida colony longer than might have otherwise been the case. McGillivray's principal commercial factor in the thriving Indian trade was the Scottish firm of Panton, Leslie and Company of Pensacola.

Jackson Oak, Daphne, Alabama.
COURTESY OF THE UNIVERSITY OF SOUTH ALABAMA ARCHIVES

The Spanish officials in Pensacola were more successful in controlling the Indians than they were in preventing the onslaught of American settlers, and the new American federal government did little to cooperate in keeping Americans at home. In 1791 Secretary of State Thomas Jefferson wrote to President Washington: "I wish 10,000 of our inhabitants would accept the invitation [to infiltrate West Florida]. It would be the means of delivering to us peacefully what might otherwise cost us a war. In the meantime, we may complain of the seduction of our inhabitants just enough to make the Spanish believe it is very wise policy for them." Events over the next two decades evolved, just as Jefferson had outlined, to bring the Gulf Coast into American hands.

It fell to Andrew Ellicott, a Quaker surveyor from Pennsylvania, to run the boundary line along the 31st parallel, as provided in the Pinckney Treaty with Spain in 1795. Part of the line ran through the large swampy area of what was soon to become Baldwin County, and Ellicott's Journal provides a colorful and graphic description of the difficult terrain in 1799. Operating in such difficult terrain, the boundary line required some three years to run, and as marked it is accurate within a few yards as determined by the most modern of surveying techniques.

As soon as the agreement had been reached with Spain regarding the border of the old southwest, the influx of settlers and a sense of urgency to establish civil government led to the creation of the Mississippi Territory in 1798. The lack of access to the sea, either down the Mississippi or the Alabama rivers, was understood to be but a temporary obstacle, and the Northwest Territory Ordinance of 1787 was used as pattern of development. In its first stage, the government was in the hands of a governor, a secretary, and three judges (all appointed by the President and confirmed by the Senate). A designated area would remain an unincorporated territory until the population reached 5,000 free adult males, at which time the voters were to be permitted to elect a territorial house of representatives, which in turn nominated ten members of the upper house. When the total population of an area reached 60,000 it could request admission as a state. Under those provisions, Alabama was a part of the Mississippi territory until 1817, and in 1819 it was admitted to statehood. Because of the rapid growth in population, Alabama passed through the territorial stage in record time, and the uncertainty of the relationship with Spanish Florida made the transition even more rapid.

Baldwin County was created during Alabama's rush to statehood, on December 21, 1809, while it was still a part of the Mississippi Territory. It was originally intended to contain not only the area between Mobile and Perdido bays, but the lower half of current Washington County along the west side of the Tombigbee as well. After several adjustments in its boundaries, Baldwin is still the largest of Alabama's counties. Reflecting the fact that many settlers of the area were from Georgia, the county was named for Abraham Baldwin, Sr., a native of Connecticut and a member of the Confederation Congress, which wrote the Constitution. Following service in the Revolution as a chaplain with the rank of Colonel, Baldwin had settled in Georgia as a member of the bar. He was also a founder of the University of Georgia and served as a member of the national House of Representatives and Senate until his death in 1807. The initial organization of Baldwin County took place in 1811, as reflected in the records of the County Court.

As settlers continued to rush to claim lands on the Gulf Coast, they began to agitate openly for free access through the Spanish West Florida to the sea—or quasi-secretly for outright annexation to the United States. Congress had jumped into the fray in 1803 by passing the Mobile Act, which added to the Mississippi customs district "all the navigable waters, rivers, creeks, bays and inlets lying within the United States which empty into the Gulf of Mexico east of the River

Mississippi." By this unilateral definition the United States seemed to have been laying claim to the lands south of the 31st parallel and between the Pearl River and Perdido Bay as a part of the Louisiana Purchase. While officials in Washington were pursuing legal and diplomatic remedies, citizen groups in Baldwin and Mobile counties were threatening direct action to seize the territory from Spain. The issue dragged on until 1813, when President Madison issued an Executive Order annexing the Pearl-Perdido area to the United States, thereby bringing all of the territory of the future Baldwin County under the control of the United States.

In Spanish East Florida, American agents were secretly working to use the threat of local uprisings as excuses to secure the territory either by purchase or outright seizure. Spain's manifest inability to defend Florida became even more crucial with the outbreak of the War of 1812, when the British occupied Pensacola and began to foment discontent among the Creek Indians. Fear overwhelmed the Gulf Coast, and military action to resolve the Florida question was seriously considered. There were international intrigues regarding West Florida, as well as domestic, but that involving Aaron Burr topped the list in potential seriousness.

Following Burr's being removed from the ticket in 1804 and his duel with Alexander Hamilton that same year, his overweening ambition drove

Aaron Burr.

him into a number of bold and dangerous undertakings. First, he plotted with General James Wilkinson to detach a large area of the trans-Mississippi West and/or Mexico in order to create his own independent nation, but his trial in Natchez did not produce sufficient evidence to convict. Hard on the heels of that escapade, after securing the promise of British support for his venture, he plunged into the backwoods of the Mississippi Territory, traveling incognito, proceeding towards Pensacola where, in all likelihood, he was preparing to meet with the Spanish Governor to lay plans to create another independent entity along the Gulf Coast. On the night of February 19, 1807, he was recognized at Washington Courthouse, was again arrested and was confined to Fort Stoddard, all the while urgently trying to communicate with Governor Galvez in Pensacola. The Administration had Burr transported under guard to stand trial before the federal District Court in Richmond, Chief Justice John Marshall presiding.

The resulting trial pitted political rivals against each other, and the potential conviction on charges of treason was blunted through the presiding judge's narrow definition of that crime, as well as the fact that highly incriminating evidence which has subsequently come to light was not available during the Burr trial. Had Burr succeeded in his plot, the entire Gulf Coast (the area including Baldwin County), might well have been included in a separate, independent nation under Burr's leadership, and he might well have enjoyed local popular support in that scheme. Wilkinson was also involved with Burr in the Gulf plot; nevertheless, after the Burr trial he sought to salvage as much as possible by leading the action against the remaining Spanish forces at Mobile on the eve of the battle of New Orleans.

No sooner had the threat of foreign intrigue been overcome than a new and even more dangerous threat of Indian unrest unsettled the Gulf Coast. As war with Britain loomed, in 1811 Chief Tecumseh of the Ohio Shawnees came south to seek an alliance with the southern tribes of Choctaw, Chickasaw, and Creek Indians. There followed several sharp battles, two of which were fought in Baldwin County, at Burnt Corn and Fort Mims. The former skirmish was fought on July 29, 1813, and it involved a clash between a group of Creeks returning from a trading voyage to Pensacola and the local militia units under the command of Colonel Collier. Immediately thereafter, the settlers in Baldwin County gathered at the stockade home of Sam Mims in northern Baldwin to meet the expected Indian counterattack. On August 30, 1813 that fateful attack came, resulting in one of the bloodiest battles in American frontier history. The losses were about 400 Indians and the massacre of about 160 settlers, including women and children. The frontier demanded retaliation and a permanent removal of the Indian threat.

Andrew Jackson was called out of early retirement to meet the Indian menace, and in 1813-1814 in several battles, culminating at Horseshoe Bend, the power of the Alabama Indian tribes was broken, their claims to lands in Alabama were removed, and the tribes themselves were ultimately relocated to western reservations. William Weatherford, or Chief Red Eagle of the Creeks, surrendered with a poignant address to Jackson. The respected chief was buried in northern Baldwin County when he died in 1824.

After the Battle of Horseshoe Bend a more hostile band of the Creeks fled to the relative safety of Spanish Florida, only to be harried again by Andrew Jackson – but an even more important threat to the stability of the Gulf Coast loomed immediately in the form of a powerful British army whose exact target was uncertain. Fear again seized the Gulf Coast, and Jackson was recalled from Florida with his militia force to check the British army. In the closing months of 1814 Jackson slowly crossed Baldwin County using the old Spanish Trail, pausing at the "Jackson Oak" in Daphne to douse the fires of rebellion in his army. He continued west, arriving at New Orleans on December 1, 1814, in time to deliver a mortal blow against the British – which was largely academic because the peace treaty had already been signed at Ghent, Belgium. Nevertheless, Jackson's victory at New Orleans removed for all time the danger of foreign or Indian intrigue along the Gulf Coast. The area was now open to being filled by American settlers; it remained only for the legal title to Spanish Florida to be obtained in the Adams-Onis Treaty of 1819. In all these momentous events, no area was more central to events than Baldwin County.

CHAPTER III

CAUGHT IN A SECTIONAL CONFLICT

The history of Baldwin County did not embrace the typical development of the Old South. It had few plantations, few slaves involved in the cultivation of cotton, and scant investment in the slavery culture of the South. Yet, in the fateful years in which sectional division tore the nation apart, it had little difficulty in deciding to which of the two systems it owed allegiance. It was Southern without being professionally so.

Baldwin was now open to the world—but still extremely difficult to reach. Surrounded by water on three sides and connected to the land mass of the United States only by miserable roads, Baldwin County posed a serious obstacle to those who wished to occupy its vast tracts of virgin land. The main overland route into the territory was the Old Federal Road, passing Fort Stoddert and Fort Mims, thence to a landing on the eastern shore of Mobile Bay near the site of the future town of Blakeley. Even the Federal Road wanted a great deal of improvement, leading an anonymous wag to post this sign along the route:

> "This road is not passable
> Not even jackassable.
> So when you travel
> Take your own gravel."

Within the area of Baldwin County, the sparse roads were even more primitive, having been built as military projects, such as the Spanish Trail, which connected Pensacola and Mobile via a ferry over the Perdido River near its mouth, thence along the route of U. S. Highway 90 through the future towns of Robertsdale and Daphne. An alternate route was the "Lower Crossing," across Perdido Bay then along a high ridge following the route of U. S. Highway 98 and Baldwin County Route 95. Using these roads, a settler might with luck cover as many as 10 miles a day, so the land journey from Pensacola to Mobile would require at least four days, while the water journey between the two ports could be made in only one day.

As settlers reached their goal, they discovered a crazy-quilt of conflicting and overlapping land titles, arising from grants from the Spanish, French, and British administrations, and purchases from the

Grand Hotel, Point Clear, Alabama.
COURTESY OF THE UNIVERSITY OF SOUTH ALABAMA ARCHIVES.

The guns of Fort Morgan, Alabama.
COURTESY OF THE UNIVERSITY OF SOUTH ALABAMA ARCHIVES.

Indians. Most settlers simply found vacant land which suited them and squatted on it, expecting that the Congress would ultimately carve up the area with rectangular survey, which actually happened in acts in 1800, 1803, and 1807. In northern Baldwin, on the banks of the Tensaw and Alabama rivers, the rich bottomland was highly prized, as were areas on the Eastern Shore near the sites of the future settlements of Aldea, Fish River, Magnolia Springs, and Bon Secour. Few grants and settlements in the interior of the county were made because of the extreme isolation of those areas. Good legal title to the whole area south of the 31st parallel was finally resolved in 1819 with the purchase of Spanish Florida, but individual land disputes continued to clog the Baldwin court system for years to come.

In the first census (1810) after Baldwin County was established, the total population was 667 white citizens and 760 blacks, for a total of 1,427. In the last census (1860) immediately prior to the Civil War, the total population was just 7,439; 3,585 whites and 3,554 blacks. These figures suggest, therefore, that there was little more than the natural increase of population for 40 years, a continuing out-migration almost matching the substantial influx of new settlers. The Atlantic Seaboard continued to provide most of the new settlers of the area, while Texas was the destination to which most of the out-migra-

tion was headed. The population statistics of Baldwin were significantly different from the counties of the Black Belt, and, while those counties went through one of the most remarkable economic booms in American history, Baldwin continued in its rather static condition.

Few settlements in the county broke the vast distances of forest and open space, but one did aspire to greatness—and for a while it did seem on its way towards reaching it. That was the Town of Blakeley, on the Tensaw River near where it empties into Mobile Bay. All that remains today of Blakeley are the dirt paths, foundations of buildings, and stately live oaks which once marked a community which rivaled Mobile in size and importance. Silting of the Tensaw River and recurring outbreaks of Yellow Fever doomed the once-thriving town. Josiah Blakeley, the father of the town, was a native of Connecticut who drifted south following the Revolution, spent several years in Cuba, and settled in Lower Alabama in 1806, then under Spanish domination. In 1813 he purchased the town site, had it incorporated, and laid out lots. Its growth was unprecedented, and within a decade the population reached 5,000, and, as the largest town in the county, it soon became the county seat.

Other than Blakeley, the only other population centers in the county were mere villages and stage stops along the principal roadways. Stage service was established along the Federal Road from Montgomery, but the high fares placed it outside the reach of all but the most affluent. Transportation was also available from Montgomery to Mobile by steamboat on the Alabama River, but, again, that level of comfort was not available to those who had nothing but their dreams to propel them.

The long, hot Baldwin summers in the days prior to air conditioning were generally a brake on the development of the Gulf Coast. Mobilians who could afford to do so usually escaped the summer heat by repairing to cottages on the Eastern Shore, from which developed a social circle given further impetus by the building of the Grand Hotel at Point Clear by F. H. Chamberlain in 1847. Although distant from the cities of the South and difficult to reach except by water, the "Grand" soon became the social scene of the South, the model for many similar establishments at a time when going on vacation to be seen by the social elite was the preferred way to relax. To many outsiders, Baldwin County and the Grand Hotel became synonymous.

For the inhabitants of the county, going to church was about the only break from the daily routine, and it was Evangelical Protestantism which appealed to the populace. The first record of a Protestant ministry in the Gulf region was the arrival of the Reverend Lorenzo Dow in 1803 in Baldwin County. Although not formally a member of the Methodist Church, Dow preached in the style of that denomination, and his efforts established the Methodist Church as one of the predominant Protestant denominations in the area. The first Protestant church was built in 1839 at Tensaw with the construction of a simple wooden chapel at Holly Creek. The Baptists first organized in the county in 1840 at Montgomery Hill, and the Episcopal Church arrived in Baldwin County with the establishment of St. Peter's Church at Bon Secour. Other church buildings were slow to materialize in the county until after the Civil War.

Public education in antebellum Alabama was given moral but little financial support, and as a consequence it languished. By the several public lands acts applicable to Baldwin County, one section out of every sixteen was supposed to be reserved for the support of public education. Unfortunately, this resource was lost in the banking panic of 1820, and, without any other support, schools in the county were generally little more than make-shift, semi-private "blab" or "old-field" establishments—and they served only a small portion of the population. The first school in the county was at Boatyard Lake in 1799, followed by Sibley Academy at Montrose in 1859. Just prior to the Civil War the county found sufficient funds to begin construction of a network of one-room schoolhouses, but operating funds permitted them to be open only a few weeks in each year. It is estimated that in 1860 approximately half of the population of the county was illiterate, and only about 3,000 students were enrolled in approximately 10 public schools.

The wide and deep popularity of Andrew Jackson in the county determined the area's political orientation for a number of years following his notable service in removing the native and foreign threats to the Gulf Coast. However, by the time of the Mexican War, Jackson's length-

ened shadow had faded, to be replaced by others of lesser stature. One such leader was William L. Yancey, a Southern "fire-eater" who more properly represented the interests of slave-owning planters of the Black Belt—but who also represented Baldwin County in the federal Congress. His hot rhetoric swept along the more moderate of his constituents, as the perpetuation of slavery was increasingly framed as a matter of Constitutional right rather than as a privilege of expansion into the western territories. Yancey was the author of an extreme manifesto presented to the Democratic Party in 1860, threatening dissolution of the Union as the preferred alternative to any compromise on the slavery issue, and when the Party rejected his views, he led the walk-out from the convention, which irrevocably split the Democratic Party and set the wheels of secession in motion. On February 24, 1860, the Alabama legislature passed an act requiring the Governor to call a secession convention if the Republican nominee were elected President, and in obedience Governor A. B. Moore convened the secession convention on December 24. Yancey was a member of the convention and was the author of the ordinance which took Alabama out of the Union. Baldwin County, with one of the lowest rates of cotton production, lowest personal wealth, smallest population, and lowest

Interior, Fort Morgan, Alabama.
COURTESY OF THE UNIVERSITY OF SOUTH ALABAMA ARCHIVES.

black populations in the state, supported the election of delegates to the Secession Convention by over 70 percent of the vote, one of the highest in the state. In the absence of any body of convincing evidence to the contrary, Baldwin County's stand on secession can only be understood in the context of following its leadership—yet in the election of 1860 Baldwin overwhelmingly supported Breckenridge, the Unionist Democratic candidate. Perhaps the political legacy of Jackson was still alive and well.

The federal census of 1860 provides a thumbnail sketch of the citizens of Baldwin County. Of the total population of just under 3,000, the area remained sparsely settled, with only two population centers at Stockton and Perdido. The listed areas of birth of a majority of the settlers were Georgia, North and South Carolina, and Scotland, and a typical household consisted of a male householder, his wife, and four children. Most indicated their calling as artisan, craftsman, or farmer, few claiming to be planters. This picture of the population suggests a rural, lower-class society with little interest in the slavery controversy, yet strongly involved because of the rhetoric of 'states' rights', which thinly covered the slavery issue.

Because of its strategic location, Baldwin County enjoyed the distinction of having a front-row seat as the war unfolded. Situated between the two critical ports of Pensacola and Mobile (the former seized early in the fighting by Union forces), Baldwin was vital to the Confederacy's goal desperately to hang on to the remaining port of Mobile, thereby making the pair of forts, Morgan and Gaines, absolutely vital. Throughout the conflict, small-scale probing operations took place in the county. It was also the site of the largest and most significant naval battle of the war, and the last land battle took place within its borders.

Immediately following Alabama's withdrawal from the Union on January 11, 1861, Governor Moore seized the forts guarding the entrance to Mobile Bay, each of which was guarded by a small detachment, but both were well supplied with stocks of powder and shot although the guns in the forts were obsolete. The Governor also revitalized the state militia organization and adopted a policy of watchfully waiting to see what the new Lincoln administration would do. The attack on Fort Sumter in Charleston harbor settled the issue.

As the ordinary private from Baldwin County reported for duty, he usually wore whatever clothing he owned, he carried a bedroll, and brought his meager personal belongings in a "gunny sack." Only some soldiers were issued uniforms, and, as the war wore on, most were forced to scrounge for replacement clothing and shoes on the battlefield. The impoverished state of the average Confederate soldier can be most graphically and pathetically read in their letters home. They freely complained of the poor food, forced marches, and cold—but hardly ever about the terrors of the battles themselves. Life was almost as bad for those they left behind at home, and they did not wish to add to the miseries of their families.

The Southern regiments were typically recruited from a single county or region, so those from Baldwin County often served in regiments from Mobile County. There is no record of artillery or cavalry units from Baldwin, but several companies of Baldwin infantry saw service as components of General Holtzclaw's Brigade, and they participated in operations in Alabama, Georgia, and Tennessee. Other Baldwin troops served as members of the 32nd Alabama Infantry in Tennessee under the command of General Nathan B. Forrest. All told, about 500 men from Baldwin County served in the Confederate Army in some of the bloodiest battles in the western theater, and less than half survived without wounds.

A perusal of the County Commission records during the war gives little clue of the hardships and privations being suffered on the home front. The first tangible response to the wartime suffering came in 1862, when the Commissioners established a program to make salt available to the families of soldiers. In that first year, a total of 790 pounds were distributed, in amounts ranging from 100 to 180 pounds per family. Also in 1862 there was established a program of emergency assistance to soldiers' families, with annual stipends ranging from $50 to $110. In that first year, a total of $33,385 was distributed to 127 destitute families, the State of Alabama reimbursing the County as it was able, up to about 75% of the total. Even with the state reimbursement, the aid to soldiers' families constituted about one-fourth of the total county budget. Because the total of Baldwin County men serving in the army at any one time was about 200, these figures indicate that a very high percentage of Baldwin County families qualified for the assistance.

Out of necessity and drawing upon the previous frontier skills of "making do," the households in Baldwin County learned to "use it up, wear it out, and when needed, do without." The Civil War was a new experience in which civilians were immediately involved and impacted, and after initially displaying ingenuity and energy those left behind on the home front found that it lost its patriotic appeal. The blockade made all things from outside the South prohibitively expensive if available at all, and substitutes had to be found for even common kitchen staples. Bicarbonate of soda used in bread-making was replaced by a slurry of burned corn cob ashes soaked in water, and coffee from South America was replaced by brews made from roasted okra seeds or parched sweet potato skins. Tea was replaced by dried berry vine leaves. The lowly ground peas, peanuts, or "goobers," that previously fed the pigs became human food. There was a continuing shortage of wheat, and Southern cooks learned to use corn meal in virtually all of their baking. Along the Gulf Coast the production of sugar cane was encouraged to replace sugar imported from Cuba, and a local variety of "ribbon cane" for making syrup became and remains a favorite

even today. Salt was in constant short supply through the war, but Baldwin fared somewhat better than other parts of the South by virtue of having salt water on three sides. At several locations along the Eastern Shore and the Gulf Coast salt ponds were dug to catch sea water from which the precious commodity was extracted.

Perhaps the most acute of all shortages was that of medical materials, forcing the households of the county to rediscover common folk remedies. Dogwood berries were found to be a substitute for quinine, the usual remedy for malaria. A solution made from blackberry roots or ripe persimmons was used for dysentery and other stomach disorders, all the more prevalent because of the unaccustomed diet. Extracts from cherry, dogwood, poplar, and wahoo trees was concocted for chills and fevers, and, for coughs, a syrup of mullein, globe flower, and wild cherry was administered. The seeds of wild castor beans were collected and pressed to make homemade castor oil.

Ordinary clothing items were scarce throughout the war, both on the battle front as well as the home front. The popular notion of the 'boys in grey' is a misnomer, for all but those newly mustered into the service wore their own civilian clothing dyed a ubiquitous brown color made of butter-nut or black walnut hulls. The uniform hat of most Southern soldiers was the same broad-brimmed slouch hat which they had worn for years in the fields at home. Shoes were a serious problem. Most of the production of leather was

Confederate earthworks,
Battle of Blakely, Alabama.
COURTESY OF BURNETTE PHOTO.

made into crude military footwear, but there were not always shoes for all the troops, and the civilian population was required to shift for themselves. By the end of the war, those on the home front generally wore slippers made of strips of worn-out clothing or carpet, and anything made of cloth was constantly recycled, cut down, let out, and reused until it was of no further value.

The Union war strategy at the outset was to capture Richmond, blockade Southern ports, and cut the Confederacy by closing the Mississippi. That spared Alabama from major battles, but the Union operations in Tennessee in 1862 dislocated thousands of refugees in that state and northern Alabama. In turn, many refugees sought safety on the vacant lands in Baldwin County. In 1863 the conflict reached the interior of Alabama, with a series of Union raids designed to break civilian morale and cripple industrial targets. In 1864 and 1865, even Lower Alabama tasted the bitter fruits of war with a series of raids, but it was in 1864 that the greatest naval engagement of the war took place in the waters off Baldwin County.

The Battle of Mobile Bay was a classic contest between attacking naval forces and defending land fortifications. It took place because Mobile was an important port of entry for the Confederacy as well as home port for the famous Confederate raiders, the CSS *Florida* and *Alabama*. In the fall of 1862 the *Florida* slipped into Mobile to finish its fitting out following construction in England, and under Captain John Moffitt it captured some 40 Union merchant ships containing goods worth more than $4 million. Of course, an even more famous Confederate raider and commander was the *Alabama* and its Captain, Raphael Semmes.

Semmes was a native of Alabama who had been a career officer in the Union Navy, last serving as inspector of lighthouses on the Gulf Coast while maintaining a home on Perdido Bay near Josephine. A daring and inventive commander, he assumed command of the Alabama fresh from her construction by Lairds Shipyard at Birkenhead, England, and, for the next two years, he and the ship terrorized Union shipping around the world until cornered at the port of Cherbourg, France. There he met his match in a battle with the USS *Kearsarge*, an even newer ship of similar design. Promoted to Rear Admiral, Semmes made his way back to the Confederacy, operated river patrol craft on the James River until Richmond was evacuated, and with no more ships to command, as a Brigadier General of Marines, led a detachment on the final march to Appomattox.

Mobile Bay was also the site of the trials of the first submarine, developed by two naval contractors from New Orleans who fled their city to Mobile in 1862. Developing their concept of a "submersible" through several models until they perfected an operating unit, the CSS Hunley was than dismantled, loaded onto rail cars, and shipped to Charleston harbor in hopes that it would be the secret weapon to break the Union blockade of that port. On its trial run in Charleston it did destroy a Union warship, but it never returned from the mission. Years afterward it was located in the harbor, raised, and the remains of the crew were honorably interred.

Mobile's location some 30 miles inland at the head of a wide and shallow bay gave it strategic importance to the political and military leaders of the North and South alike. Second only to New Orleans, it was the best port on the Gulf Coast, with rail lines and navigable waterways running into the interior. Southern expectations of winning the economic struggle by the continued export of cotton made keeping it open despite the Union blockade an absolute necessity, while the inconclusive results of the blockade made its outright capture a Union imperative. The narrow entrance to Mobile Bay was guarded by the twin forts, Gaines and Morgan, and a forced entry into the bay could not be effected until a substantial land army was available to support it. That gave the South three years of extremely valuable, relatively free entry, during which time more than $2,000,000 in cotton was exported and an even larger amount of critical goods were imported. Of the total number of ships attempting to run the Mobile blockade, it is estimated that about 80 percent were successful. Union pride demanded the capture of Mobile, but it was summer of 1864 before sufficient force could be brought together. The opposing commanders were Confederate Admiral Franklin Buchanan, a native of Maryland who had cast his lot with the South, and Admiral David Farragut, a Southerner who elected to remain in the Union service.

Farragut had the larger fleet, a motley collection of old wooden sailing vessels and modern steam-propelled ones, while Buchanan had a smaller fleet featuring several ironclads, which were aptly described as "hastily-constructed of green timbers with sheets of iron slapped upon their sides." However, the ironclads had the psychological advantage as a newer weapon. Besides, Buchanan had the support of the batteries of the two forts and a prepared mine field, then referred to as "torpedoes." What he lacked was the fighting spirit of his adversary. In late May, 1864, the Confederate ram Tennessee reached the lower bay and anchored off Fort Morgan. Farragut expected that Buchanan was preparing to try a break-out before his fleet was ready to push into the bay, and he went on full alert. Against his own scruples, he even decided to use torpedoes as a counter-measure in the forthcoming engagement. Buchanan hesitated, so by August 5, Farragut decided to attack.

At dawn the wind blew steadily from the southwest, forming a natural screen to carry the battle smoke to Fort Morgan's batteries. Farragut formed his ships in a double column, ironclads and steam vessels on the right closest to the fort, while the older, wooden vessels formed a line on the left, shielded as much as possible from Fort Morgan's guns. The lead vessel in the left column was the Brooklyn, under the command of Captain James Alden, followed by the flagship, the Hartford, in which Farragut had himself lashed to the rigging the better to observe and command the operation. Shortly after the beginning of the battle, Captain Alden signaled that he had slowed to keep from overrunning the ironclad column. Farragut immediately replied, "Order the monitors ahead, and go on." Shortly after that, Farragut watched in horror as the lead ironclad, Tecumseh, struck a mine and quickly settled by the bow, taking all but 20 members of the crew with her. Unless aggressive action had been taken, the battle might well have gone to the defenders, but Farragut seized the initiative and signaled the fleet to follow him. The famous quotation said to have been issued at this time, "Damn the torpedoes! Full speed ahead!" was not uttered by Farragut at this time or any other during the battle, but it was actually an invention of a newspaper reporter some fourteen years later to give additional color to the battle. In the confusion of the crucial period in the battle, what the Admiral did ask his signalman, "Can you say 'For God's sake' by signal?" "Yes, Sir," was the reply. "Then say to the Lackawanna, "For God's sake get out of the way and anchor!" In his haste the signalman dropped the signal staff on the Admiral's head, causing him to wince—but history did not record anything he may have said at that juncture.

At the end of the battle, the Union fleet had lost the Tecumseh and the supply ship Phillipi, with damage to several others. The Confederate fleet was scattered, and the Tennessee was out of commission and forced to surrender with the commanding Admiral. The most important result was that the entrance to Mobile Bay had been breached, and Mobile was removed as a functioning port. Total Union casualties were 52 killed and 170 wounded, and the total Confederate losses were 12 killed, 20 wounded, and 280 captured. Several days later Fort Morgan was forced to surrender, and Mobile awaited its fate.

Even after Federal forces controlled the entrance to the bay, Mobile remained in Confederate hands for a few more months. Early in January, 1865, General E. S. R. Canby began a slow pincer movement along both sides of Mobile Bay until the low ground south of Mobile caused him to concentrate his force on the east side of the Bay. The entire Union force numbered about 45,000 and it moved against Confederate defenders numbering not more than 3,000, but the difficulty of crossing the Delta at the north end of the Bay worked to the advantage of the defenders. After a skirmish at Spanish Fort on March 27, a pitched battle was fought at Blakeley on April 19. The Confederates, short of food and ammunition and reduced to sending under-age boy reserves of 15 and 16 into battle, were overwhelmed by a force more than 10 times larger. About 2,000 slain from both sides were buried in a mass grave, and 3,423 Confederates were taken prisoner, all in vain, since, unknown at the time, General Lee had already effectively ended the war with the surrender at Appomattox Court House. War-weary, a stillness hung over the once-pleasant land of Baldwin County, as its people waited to see what new trials the end of fighting in the terrible war would bring.

CHAPTER IV

RECONSTRUCTION AND TIMBER EXPLOITATION

❖

The steamer Fairhope, *part of the fleet which formerly plied Mobile Bay, 1900.*
COURTESY OF THE UNIVERSITY OF SOUTH ALABAMA ARCHIVES.

The Confederacy was militarily defeated long before the last shots were fired, but even more important, the psychology of defeat had eroded the Southern political and social fabric for months prior to the last battles. While some areas indulged the fantasy of guerilla resistance, and some social groups preferred to emigrate rather than accept their fate, most of Baldwin's population was simply too tired and bankrupt to do anything other than to fall back on their rural self-sufficiency, pull up their boot straps, and contemplate the cause of their misery.

Whatever might have happened had Lincoln lived to preside over the re-unification of the nation, the practical reality was that the Southern political system had simply ceased to function. At the grass-roots level, did the judges and other political office-holders in Baldwin County have any valid claim to office? Just who was to repair and lead a broken political system? A total population of just over 6,000 in 1870 (2,845 black and 3,159 white) did not know where to look for answers. Over 1,000 former slaves in the county had simply disappeared since the 1860 census.

There is no statistical index of the poverty of Baldwin County in 1865, but even after a few years of recuperation the picture was still bleak. In 1870 the county then had only 4,919 acres of improved land under cultivation, more than 70,000 acres having been abandoned to weeds. Good land was generally available at $2.00 per acre, and the total agricultural production of the county was only $81,000. Blakeley, Stockton, and Montgomery Hill were noted in the 1870 as "small villages;" otherwise, the county was officially declared "a vast pine forest, with numerous lumber mills." At a meeting of the County Commission in 1865, the County Treasurer solemnly reported that there were "no funds in the county treasury, and no income [was] likely for the next twelve months." In desperation, to keep the essential functions of police and administration of justice in operation, the Sheriff was authorized to borrow $2,000 at interest not to exceed ten percent, and, for the next several years, the entire budget for the County did not exceed $5,000. Most county landowners could not pay even their very meager tax bills, and no effort was made to collect except from large corporations.

The process of political Reconstruction followed different patterns in each Southern state and county. In the Alabama Black Belt, where the planter aristocracy was thought to have forfeited its right to leadership, local office holders were summarily removed, but in counties such as Baldwin, which had no entrenched aristocracy, the incumbents were allowed to remain in office until natural rotation had its effect. Under the terms of Presidential Reconstruction in 1865, the new Provisional Governor issued proclamations which retained in office all those who could and would take an oath of allegiance. When a constitutional convention was called to convene in 1865, J. H. Hastie, a moderate, represented Baldwin County. The convention did not seek to define the status of the freed slaves, but it did reject a move to extend to them the suffrage. After the convention had finished its work, the new state constitution was declared in force by a vote of 61 to 25, without a vote of the people. The work of the 1865 convention was generally considered to have been merely "putting a new face on the old system," and the Radical Republicans in Congress were having none of it. The Alabama Reconstruction Legislature, which met in January 1866, further aggravated the issue by passing the so-called "Black Code," which purported to regulate the status of the former slaves in ways virtually indistinguishable from their former condition under the law. The answer to such obdurate conduct was the passage of the Civil Rights Act, over the veto of President Johnson, which declared that all persons born within the United States were citizens and entitled to all the rights and privileges thereof, and the passage of the Reconstruction Acts of 1867, which placed the former southern states under military rule.

Political chicanery based on race has been said to be a peculiarly Alabama political art; if so, it was born in the Reconstruction Era. The Reconstruction Acts of 1867 provided that only those who could take the "iron-clad" oath that they had never voluntarily served the Confederacy could be placed on the new voter rolls, the administrators of which were federal army officers. In Baldwin County, most of the black population but less than half of the white males were registered, and the members of the constitutional convention they elected were mostly without property, ignorant or politically inexperienced, and under the direction of others. Radical concepts incorporated in the new constitution were: universal manhood suffrage; universal public education; an expanded militia system (presumably a guarantee against an effort by white rebels to seize the government); and establishment of several new local political offices (presumably a training ground for those without political experience). When submitted to referendum by the voters, it was adopted 70,000 to 1,000.

Despite a white boycott, the total votes cast were several thousand less than a majority of those registered. It could be argued that the Constitution of 1868 was not legally adopted, but it was the price of re-admission to the Union.

It was now the turn of the white men of Alabama to resort to intimidation and violence in the effort to regain control of the state, and the instrument of choice was the Ku Klux Klan. It had been founded in Pulaski, Tennessee, in 1866, and it quickly found its way into Alabama, where it widely employed the tactics of intimidation and violence without leaving much of a record in Baldwin County. Alabama Republicans did what they could by passing legislation outlawing the Klan's activities, but an organization based upon secrecy was inherently difficult to detect and control. During Radical Reconstruction the Radicals may have ruled in the State House, but the Klan more often than not ruled the backwoods. The Reconstruction government of Alabama was corrupt and ineffective, and it spent far more than current revenue collections, leaving a crushing load of public debt at the state and local level. It sponsored a wild spree of railroad construction, and gave little attention to other pressing public needs. But it did establish the foundation of a public education system, albeit on a segregated basis. In 1870 the report of the state Superintendent of Public Instruction claimed there were 13 white schools in Baldwin County and four black schools, enrolled about 20,000 white children and 15,000 black ones, at a cost of about $5,000 annually.

Fairhope, Alabama, ice plant.
COURTESY OF THE UNIVERSITY OF SOUTH ALABAMA ARCHIVES.

Reconstruction also left a strong political legacy in the form of Bourbon Democracy, the label which the reconstructed Democrats adopted when they regained control of the political system. The term recalls the Bourbon regime in France, the members of which were said never to have forgotten anything old nor learned anything new. In Alabama it referred to a party which was dedicated to antebellum ideals of limited government and frugality, modified by a broader popular base of political participation, reducing the public debt of the Reconstruction Era, and the ideal of public honesty in government, even if that goal were marred by occasional incidents of corruption. In Baldwin County, as in many of the counties, the coalition between the conservative Bourbons and nascent Populism was held together by the common ground of the race issue. That coalition came apart in the 1890s, when the Bourbons too long ignored pressing social and fiscal issues.

The election of 1874 in which the Bourbons finally wrested control of the state from the Radicals is regarded as one of the most corrupt in the history of the state. A simple yet forceful concept was developed, involving a complete takeover of all levels of control on the basis of what was termed the Pike County platform. Intimidation, rioting, theft of ballots, and assassination were all employed. The federal troops in the state, only some 1,000 strong, were powerless to prevent the coup, and the newly-elected Bourbon Governor called for a new convention to rewrite the state constitution. In the ensuing election, many citizens of Florida "crossed the line" to

Baldwin and other adjacent counties to push the totals to the required level. The resulting new constitution pushed the clock back to the status of 1865, and for the next 30 years the Bourbons ran Alabama. In Baldwin County that meant that the County Commission largely occupied itself with building roads and bridges at minimal expense, often charging tolls on critical passageways, or authorizing private citizens to do the same things. A "public roadway" was defined as any route open to members of the public who were willing to brave dirt, washouts, high water, and fallen trees. It was usually a single-tract, unimproved, ill-marked, and miserable excuse for a road.

The Achilles heel of Bourbon democracy was its treatment of prisoners, especially the practice of hiring out on contract the state and some county prison inmates. Because of the manifest abuses in the system, the Bourbons were vulnerable on the issue, and the crusade to change the system resulted in other social reforms as by-products. In consequence, Baldwin created a County Home for the destitute, populated only by blacks, since no self-respecting white citizen would permit himself to take advantage of the institution. Strange as it may seem, the Bourbons were responsible for creating the best public health system in the South, based upon making the medical practitioners in each county the de facto board of public health. By such means, the recurring outbreaks of Yellow Fever in coastal communities were finally brought under control, and Baldwin County was often visited by groups from other states studying the effective means of disease control.

Having little if anything to do with Bourbon politics, there was a concerted effort in the late nineteenth century to "correct" the mistake which history and international intrigue had made in leaving the area south of the 31st parallel and east of the Perdido, the Panhandle, as a part of Florida. The Bourbon effort to recapture the Panhandle was made primarily for the benefit of Alabama's business and industrial leaders, to provide a second port for Alabama's expanding international trade. In 1869 commissioners of the two states agreed on the terms of the cession, but the Alabama legislature refused to ratify because it did not have the funds required for the purchase. Again, in 1873, the Alabama legislature appropriated $1,000,000 to complete the purchase, but that time Florida refused to approve the deal. Pensacola strongly favored the deal, as did Baldwin County. Had it been consummated, it would have resulted in a powerful boost to the regional economy. That did not happen, but at least the Bourbons tried.

The economy of Baldwin County in the last third of the nineteenth century was largely dominated by the land boom and lumbering, large tracts being offered for sale at about $1.25 per acre by out-of-state land and lumber companies which had bought the acres for nominal amounts either from the government or at tax sales during the Reconstruction Era. Baldwin remained off the beaten tract, sparsely populated, without visible attractions except for its innumerable trees. Prior to the Civil War there had been no practical way to transport such a bulky commodity as lumber to market, or the depressed market for the product left it without a ready sale. Some limited production had been developed in naval stores, but that was limited to a local market in Pensacola or Mobile. The rapid change in the national economy following the war changed all that. Now it became feasible to fell Baldwin pine, cut it into lumber, load it on sailing vessels, and transport it at a profit to markets on the Eastern Seaboard or Europe—but what was left was cut-over land which was worthless except as the site for farms at the cost of back-breaking work. Sale of such cut-over land was limited to relative newcomers who for whatever reason preferred to clear the fields of Baldwin to breaking the plains of Nebraska. Beginning in the 1890s those economic forces resulted in the doubling of the county's population about every decade and the attraction of essentially new cultural groups to create a new mix of cultures.

The second significant impact the timber boom had on Baldwin was that for once the area had a cash crop to sell. Even though the profit was largely drained off to out-of-state, corporate owners, substantial money was infused into the local economy in the form of wages and local spending. That provided the basis of a very rapid expansion of retail trade in the county.

Once the lumber barons began to taste the profits pine trees could generate, they began to urge, even demand, an improvement in the transportation facilities to facilitate the movement of lumber to market. Because of the bulky nature of the commodity and the need to con-

Hunter's cabin, Elberta, Alabama.
COURTESY OF THE UNIVERSITY OF SOUTH ALABAMA ARCHIVES.

centrate saw mills in a few locations, the felled logs were usually hauled or floated to the mills located on or near the waterways surrounding the county, from which the lumber could be loaded on ships. Typical was the large forested area on the western shore of Perdido Bay. During the winter months, laborers would clear-cut the pine, filling the air with clouds of thick smoke as the slash and tops were burned where they fell. The massive logs were dragged by oxen to the closest watercourse or dug canals to await the spring rains to swell the water to sufficient depth to float the logs down to the Perdido. The logs of each company would be marked with the owner's distinctive marking, and gangs of "timber cowboys" would sort and guide them to the several saw mills lining the shores of Perdido Bay. The resulting lumber was loaded onto fleets of old sailing vessels for delivery to markets on the Eastern Seaboard.

The same water and rail links which were developed to transport lumber to the outside world also served to bring waves of new settlers to till the new ground once it had been cleared of trees. What the timber companies sold as "prime agricultural lands" was several years of hard labor in the making, and the county was regarded as so remote that the companies had to resort to high-pressure tactics and foreign countries to find their sales. All that was missing for the county to realize its potential was the flood of people to populate its vast, unoccupied spaces, turning Baldwin County from a timber preserve to a patchwork of farms.

CHAPTER V

IMMIGRATION AND AGRICULTURE

In 1890 the population of Baldwin County was 8,941; in 1900 it had grown to 13,194; and ten years later it had grown to over 17,000. It has continued to grow ever since at an accelerating rate greater than that of Alabama as a whole. In a nutshell, those population trends constitute the theme of Baldwin's history in the twentieth century. In this era the boom in Baldwin was in people.

It is difficult to imagine the primitive conditions of life in Baldwin County even as late as the 1880s and 1890s, but a first-person account of the conditions will suffice to make the point. Writing in 1881, a young woman who had only recently arrived left this account of life in the pine woods: "The house was 9 by 14 feet and had not a window or door shutter. There was a large new fireplace and that pleased me more than anything else. We had not had a yard fence for a long time; therefore, we could not keep a dog. I have often wondered that the wild animals did not tear me to pieces as I was alone part of the time and my nearest neighbor was three miles away."

"I found that the greater number of people here had lived just the same. There was no reading matter to be had, as the nearest post office was twenty miles away. There was a period of three years that I did not see a printed article except my Bible. I read it for company, read it for pastime, read it for consolation in my many lonely hours."

In addition to the sheer numbers of those who found their way to the county, the new settlers stimulated the growth of a number of towns. Bay Minette, shortly to be stimulated by the relocation of the county seat, was founded in 1908 by J. D. Hand, and it quickly grew to a population of 2,000. Foley, founded by the Chicago druggist John B. Foley, quickly swelled to 800, and Fairhope had a population of 1,500 within twenty years of its establishment. The census of 1920 counted a total county population of just over 20,000.

The founding and development of the town of Foley illustrates how Baldwin was often promoted, as well as the close cooperation between economic interests in 'boosting' Baldwin settlement. In 1901, Colonel J. M. Green, a land agent for the L. & N. Railroad, was traveling to Washington for the funeral of President William McKinley. On the trip he met the Chicago manufacturing druggist,

John Burton Foley. Green waxed enthusiastically about the attractions of Baldwin County, and the next year Foley paid a visit to the area to see for himself. He was impressed and purchased a tract of 40,000 acres of prime, virgin timberland in the name of the Magnolia Springs Land Company, and he employed agents who traveled through the midwest to sell farms to settlers.

Foley perceived that easier transport was needed to facilitate land sales to his prospects, so he proposed to build a branch line south from Bay Minette if the L. & N. would operate it. A deal was struck, even including the provision of wood fuel from one of Foley's sawmills for the locomotives on the line. Prospects were welcomed by burning torches at homes along the right-of-way, and every effort was made to make them feel welcome. Shortly after purchasing their land, the newcomers would return bringing their furniture and farm equipment with them in a boxcar. By 1921 Foley boasted many new brick buildings, a drug store with an ornate soda fountain, a general grocery, a meat processing plant, a general dry-goods store, a cotton gin, an electric generating plant, a fertilizer plant, a tin shop, a fish market, a greenhouse, a new addition to the Magnolia Hotel, and a new telephone system. In that same year it shipped 250 carloads of lumber, salted fish, and citrus fruit.

The tide of immigration was only beginning. Newcomers from many ethnic and national origins were recruited to find homes in Baldwin, making it an area of cultural diversity.

The first immigrant group to settle in Baldwin was the Italian colony in Daphne in 1888. In that year Alesandro Mastro Valerio bought a tract of land on which to locate a colony for his countrymen who were not thriving in the crowded urban areas of America. He devoted some fourteen of his later years to making a success of the undertaking, employing scientific truck farming methods. The first members of the colony to arrive were Domenico Trione and the Castagnolli brothers, and they were later joined by twenty additional families recruited from the Chicago area. Each family purchased 25 to 50 acres at an average price of $1.50 to $5.00 an acre, on which they grew tobacco, rice, sweet and Irish potatoes, wheat, cotton, and truck vegetables. In time production shifted to potatoes and green corn because those crops seemed to thrive best

in Baldwin's soil and climate. Soon after their arrival, the Italian colony built the Church of the Assumption, and Fr. Angelo Chiariaglione arrived in 1897 to serve the parish. Known for his many acts of charity and civic promotion, he was beloved and respected by parishioners and neighbors alike. At his death in 1908 he was buried in the courtyard of the church he had served so faithfully.

A second colony established on the Eastern Shore was by a group of followers of Henry George. The essence of George's philosophy was that all land values increase as a result of society's actions, thus the increase is not earned or merited by the landowner. To recapture the unearned increase in land values the disciples of George held property in common, renting their allotted portion from the community, while paying a "single tax" to the community sufficient to

Above: July 4th celebration, Magnolia Springs, Alabama.
COURTESY OF THE UNIVERSITY OF SOUTH ALABAMA ARCHIVES.

Below: Residential street in Fairhope, Alabama.
COURTESY OF THE UNIVERSITY OF SOUTH ALABAMA ARCHIVES.

NEW YEAR'S DAY 1914 AT BIDE-A-WEE, FOLEY, ALA. WINTER HOME OF H.P. FLINT.

Above: A rude cabin at Foley, Alabama, 1914.
COURTESY OF THE UNIVERSITY OF SOUTH ALABAMA ARCHIVES.

Below: Orange Beach, Alabama, before modern development.
COURTESY OF THE UNIVERSITY OF SOUTH ALABAMA ARCHIVES.

pay ordinary land tax and other public services. In order for such a radical departure from usual American land-holding practice to succeed, a colony needed to be isolated in a virgin area, peopled exclusively by those who subscribed to the concept. The group investigated the Eastern Shore through the efforts of E. Q. Norton of Daphne, and it purchased a block of 150 acres with bay front at $6.00 per acre. The first group of the colony arrived on November 15, 1894, from Minnesota, Ohio, Pennsylvania, British Columbia, and Missouri, all socially and politically progressive and all answering to the term, 'mild Socialists.' Other Baldwin residents called the Fairhope colonists a 'bunch of crazy Yankees with some crazy ideas." Although the Fairhope colony differed radically from the prevailing norms of Baldwin County, it grew rapidly. The colony purchased more land on which to expand, and it attracted new settlers, including

a group of Quakers. From the outset the Fairhope community exhibited a high regard for education, and an experimental school was one of the first buildings constructed by the colony.

The area of Baldwin which attracted a Scandinavian settlement was known as Silverhill, west of Robertsdale. The name originated because the owner of a store in that vicinity insisted on being paid in silver instead of paper currency. To this area in 1897 came Oscar Johnson, C. O. Carlson, and C. D. Valentine, all of Chicago, to create a prosperous settlement of Scandinavians concentrating on dairying and truck farming to serve the Mobile market. Johnson made his own home in his colony, and he made his own contribution by the introduction of Satsuma oranges to the county. In 1904 A. A. Norden moved from Omaha to Silverhill to establish an early traveler's hotel, supposedly the foundation of the tourism industry in the county. In 1909 the Silverhill community was enriched by the arrival of a group of Bohemian families, and by 1926 Silverhill was incorporated as a town with a population of over 400 families.

Germans were added to the ethnic mix in 1905 when the Baldwin County Colonization Company was formed to sell cut-over land around Elberta. More than 53,000 acres in that area was owned by the Southern States Lumber Company, and finding insufficient interest among American buyers, the Company looked for purchasers in Germany. The first step was to build roads at company expense along the section lines, and one-room schoolhouses were constructed at two or three mile intervals. About 500 families were recruited, about half Lutheran and half Catholic, to settle in the area.

In 1906 a sister company to the Southern States brought 43 families of Polish descent to settle on lands in and around Summerdale. Excellent farmers, the Polish colonists flourished in Baldwin, but within a generation their descendants scattered to other areas of the county or were assimilated into the general population.

In many respects the most remarkable ethnic group to locate in Baldwin County were the Greek colonists who came to Malbis. The story of its origin hangs on the travels of a young Greek philanthropist, Jason Malbis, who visited the United States to determine the status of Greek immigrants. He found some in distress but others pros-

ORANGE BEACH, ALA.

pering, but for all he wished to offer the opportunity of preserving their own culture and religion. While Malbis was visiting in Mobile he happened to purchase a watermelon which had been grown in Baldwin County, and he was so struck by the quality of the fruit that he decided on the spot to purchase two sections of land northeast of Daphne on which to locate a religious Greek colony. The result was a prosperous settlement, largely based on providing high-quality food for Mobile. Malbis ultimately became a memorial to all the Greek in America, with a beautiful Orthodox basilica as a memorial to Malbis and all Greek-Americans. It is a major tourist attraction in the county.

Although now largely dispersed, a group of French-Canadians in 1909, led by F. X. Duchesneau of Montreal came to Baldwin County. He originally selected Fairhope as the preferred area, but after 1911 a second wave came to join the vanguard and settled in the Elsanor area. These settlers ran truck farms to supply the food markets of Pensacola.

Prodded by the political and religious unrest in their homelands prior to the outbreak of World War I, in 1913 a group of Croatians, or Jugoslavs, migrated to form a settlement at Perdido. They had come originally to Illinois, Missouri, Colorado, and Wisconsin to work in the mines, but now wished to escape the dangers of that calling. Taking advantage of the deep, rich soil of Baldwin County, they turned to growing Irish and sweet potatoes through a marketing cooperative which they formed.

One of the last colonies to be established in Baldwin was an Amish group near Bay Minette about 1915. The group was known as Hooker Mennonites because they used hooks and eyes instead of buttons on their clothing. The group had originally settled in Kansas, later removed to Arizona, but still later sought land in Alabama for greater isolation. They supported themselves by general farming, poultry raising, and extracting turpentine.

All of the ethnic groups which arrived in Baldwin about the same time brought with them not only cultural diversity but the most current

Above: A typical "dog trot" cabin near Stockton, Alabama, 1890.
COURTESY OF THE UNIVERSITY OF SOUTH ALABAMA ARCHIVES.

Below: A fishing party, Fairhope, Alabama, 1895.
COURTESY OF THE UNIVERSITY OF SOUTH ALABAMA ARCHIVES.

There is good fishing in Mobile Bay at Fairhope, Alabama

❖

A wading party, Sweetwater, Alabama.
COURTESY OF THE UNIVERSITY OF SOUTH
ALABAMA ARCHIVES

"Railroad Bill—mighty bad man,
Shoot dem lights out de brakeman's han'
When was lookin' fo' Railroad Bill."

It is unclear exactly what was the reason for Morris Slater's anger against the L. & N., but about 1893 this black turpentine worker came out of the pine woods to Atmore, armed and with blood in his eye. When challenged by a policeman in Atmore, Slater shot the officer, caught a freight train, and became a fugitive. For years he made a practice of breaking open cases of canned goods and throwing the contents out to unfortunates along the railroad right-of-way. Whenever he was pursued too closely he fought back, running up a total of 15 killings. His capture became the standard campaign promise for years for every sheriff in Lower Alabama. The L. & N. offered a reward of $1,250 and a lifetime pass to anyone providing information leading to Bill's capture, and in 1896 the reward was collected by Leonard McGowin, who shot Bill while he was shopping in Atmore. The railroad had his body embalmed and placed on public display in order to dispel the myth of Bill's immortality.

Had there been any banks in Baldwin County, perhaps Railroad Bill might have become a bank robber in the more classical tradition of the frontier. It may be difficult to imagine, but for the first century of Baldwin's existence there was not a single bank within its borders. The first to be chartered was the Baldwin County Bank in 1902, at Bay Minette, with a capital of $15,000. Until the Depression it was still the largest. The Robertsdale Bank was second, chartered in 1911 with a capital of $40,000. The Bank of Fairhope was third in 1917, with $16,000 in capital. All of these early banks prospered and greatly expanded their capital within a decade. These figures of bank growth prove the general economic growth of the county and that most of the profit from the various forms of endeavor remained in the county.

The addition of the several ethnic strains to the Baldwin population also gave it something of a cultural and literary tradition which it might not otherwise have had, one of celebrating itself through authors drawing upon local lore to spin tales with realistic details. This school of writing, sometimes called "slack-jaw realism," flourished in

of scientific farm practices, and they laid the foundations for an agricultural boom which has continued until the present. The combination of deep sandy loam with clay sub-soil, adequate rainfall, and an enlightened work force worked miracles. In the 1920s, with less than ten percent of the arable land in the county actually under cultivation, significant profits were realized from the scientific "book-farming." For example, in 1926 in the county there were slightly more than 3,500 acres of satsuma oranges producing an income of in excess of $100,000. Before being displaced by central and south Florida, Baldwin County led the nation in the production of citrus fruit, most of which was processed and packed in a large complex of warehouses adjacent to the L. & N. Rail line in Foley. Another important crop was pecans, a paper-shell variety having been developed in Baldwin through grafting. Sweet and Irish potatoes valued at over $2,250,000 were shipped each year in the decade of the 1920s.

The branch line to Foley played a major role in the agricultural boom, but it also served to provide local color as well. As the James Brothers and other notorious outlaws took out their anger on the rail lines in the far west, so too did a character with the colorful name of "Railroad Bill" terrorize the rails in Baldwin for a number of years. There was even a popular ballad written to celebrate his exploits:

many parts of the post-war South, but there was an especially rich vein which was originally seen in the columns of local Baldwin newspapers. One might wonder what newly-arrived immigrants must have made of 'possoms which talked, bull-frogs which sang grand opera, and the antics of Railroad Bill, but that is exactly what they found in the pages of such local papers as the Badlwin Times (Bay Minette), The Onlooker (Foley), the Courier (Fairhope), and the Baldwin County News (Foley). In opening their pages to the local amateur writers, the local papers encouraged the growth of a local tradition of tale-telling which preserved a great deal of local color which would have otherwise been lost forever. That tradition is still alive, perhaps best seen in the enormously successful novel and motion picture by Harper Lee entitled To Kill a Mockingbird. Set in neighboring Monroe County, the story might as will have been a reflection of Baldwin County had there been a Baldwin Harper Lee to write it.

The nineteenth century ended and the twentieth began with the Spanish-American War, which was a watershed for the nation as well as for the county. Prior to the war, Baldwin had been at the end of the line, the last stop before American culture was lost in a stew of Caribbean flavors. But this war, precisely because of its locale, suddenly shifted the geographical axis and the former last stop suddenly became an attic window overlooking the rest of the world. Previously, if they worried about such matters at all, Baldwin citizens worried about transportation improvements tying the area to the rest of the nation. Thereafter, they dreamed about capitalizing on their location astride an avenue of international commerce and the projection of American power beyond American shores. An Alabama senator, John Tyler Morgan, had for years been preaching the message of American expansionism, and now at last his constituents, especially those in Mobile and Baldwin counties, caught the message.

What the war produced was a new American empire. Suddenly, the flag waved above Cuba,

Above: A ferry over Fish River.
COURTESY OF THE UNIVERSITY OF SOUTH ALABAMA ARCHIVES.

Below: New Baldwin County
Courthouse, Bay Minette, Alabama.
COURTESY OF THE UNIVERSITY OF SOUTH ALABAMA ARCHIVES.

as well as the Philippines, Puerto Rico, and Guam—and places with such a favorable situation as Baldwin dreamed of new markets for the products of its farms and forests. A new surge of national pride swelled, and the county eagerly supported the expansion of the navy to protect the empire. A rising tide was expected to float all boats.

Along the Gulf Coast, tides are not all that occasionally rise—at times to record heights. As a larger population and more development was exposed to the recurring hurricanes, greater

damage was to be expected. One such storm was that of September 27, 1907, when tides more than 15 feet above normal were recorded. In Baldwin County alone the storm beached 35 vessels, sank 14 boats, and approximately fifty additional small craft were left damaged or beyond repair. The devastation was especially severe near Fort Morgan, near Navy Cove, where a tidal wave of immense proportion swept over the sand spit, changing forever the landscape. A total of 14 buildings was partially or totally destroyed, and the loss of life was contained only by the superior seamanship of the community. Another massive storm hit Baldwin on July 5, 1916, and winds in excess of 100 miles per hour and a tidal surge of over 12 feet was recorded. On this occasion the storm came shore near Gulfport, Mississippi, remaining stationary over Alabama from July 6 to 10, killing 13 and producing damage in excess of $3.5 million on the Alabama coast alone.

One of the more bizarre stories of Baldwin's past at the turn of the century was the battle of the courthouses, complete with the threat of mob action and armed conflict. The first county seat was at McIntosh on the Tombigbee River, when Baldwin was first created. Next the county seat was moved to Blakeley in 1810, when that village was in a race with Mobile for importance as a port. In 1898 the state legislature moved the county seat to the largest town, Daphne, and a new masonry court house was built to house it until secret negotiations between the city fathers of Bay Minette and the L. & N. Railway resulted in a hasty relocation to the latter town. Daphne was prepared to fight to defend its rights by force of arms, but trickery prevailed and the county records were loaded on oxcarts and transported to Bay Minette, where a new structure was built in 1901 on land donated by the L. & N.

The twin public concerns which occupied the attention of the County Commission between the two world wars were getting the county roads paved and public education. Only the main highways crossing the county received pavement until the 1930s, and a network of one-room schools answered the needs of public education in the rural portions of the county.

 Top, left: Main Entrance, Baldwin County Courthouse, Bay Minette.

COURTESY OF BURNETTE PHOTO.

Top, right: Historical marker, courthouse, Bay Minette, Alabama.

COURTESY OF BURNETTE PHOTO.

Below: The former courthouse, Daphne, Alabama.

COURTESY OF THE UNIVERSITY OF SOUTH ALABAMA ARCHIVES.

CHAPTER VI

WORLD WAR II AND THE BEGINNING OF TOURISM

The municipal pier, Fairhope, Alabama.
COURTESY OF THE UNIVERSITY OF SOUTH
ALABAMA ARCHIVES.

As most American farmers were struggling through the 1920s with over-production and declining prices, the experience of those of Baldwin County was significantly more favorable. Baldwin farmers had largely switched from depressed staple crops to those less so, such as truck farming, soybeans, snap beans, pecans, and sweet and Irish potatoes. In Baldwin County growing pecans also went hand-in-hand with raising cattle due to the extensive pasture area between the trees. Until 1945, Baldwin cattle were allowed to wander on the open range, but thereafter mandatory fencing of pasture required cattlemen to upgrade their herds. In the years immediately prior to World War II, the county supported over 50,000 head of cattle, most of superior quality.

Baldwin forests continued to contribute to the gross income of the county in good years as well as lean, but as the boom in saw timber slowed in the 1920s, the expansion of other forest products such as pulp wood, pilings, utility poles, and logs for plywood manufacture more than offset the decline. In the 1920s Baldwin farmers also began to see the economic advantages in replanting their forests, and by the 1930s there was actually an increase in the acres of timber in growth.

The productive waters surrounding the county have also provided an important source of income for Baldwin citizens, shifting from what might be called "subsistence fishing" around 1900 to full-scale commercial fishing by the 1930s. Using the rail spur to Foley as a shipping point, it became possible for local fisheries to supply oysters, shrimp, and fish to an expanding market. For example, in 1900 some 600 barrels of oysters were taken in each week of the season (September through April), but that harvest continued to expand even in the Depression, and by the 1930s the weekly take had grown to several thousand barrels. The same was true of the shrimp harvest. Fresh flounder, red snapper, grouper, mullet, and other Gulf species added their value to the total fisheries fame and income of the county, now exceeding $40,000,000 per year. The productivity of Baldwin fisheries had been significantly enhanced by a program of creating artificial reefs in the Gulf, which lure fish to those locales.

An anomaly of fishing in Baldwin County is the occasional "Jubilee," when one does not need to fish for creatures of the sea; instead, they literally jump out of the water and catch themselves for those who happen to be along the Eastern Shore when the conditions are right. The phenomenon is not fully understood, but it is associated with the depletion of oxygen in the bay water in summer and an east wind blowing off the cliffs along the shore. When those conditions prevail, the fruits of the sea literally fight to jump out of the water onto the shore and may be scooped up to enjoy.

Getting Baldwin County "out of the mud" and better connected to the rest of the nation continued to be a major goal of county government and a key to the growth of the economy in the 1920s and 1930s. Bridging the water which surrounds the county was not an easy task; Mobile Bay was crossed by the Cochran Bridge, and a one-lane wooden span over Perdido Bay in the eastern side of the county was built just prior to World War I. Both links were expensive, but both were imperative to the economic development of the county. Paving the principal roadways in the county was also an expensive undertaking, but a beginning was made in 1927 with the designation of the roads with the highest priority.

During the 1920s several business interests along the Gulf Coast began to agitate for the development of an interior canal for barge traffic, and the Baldwin section of the project was completed in 1930 at a total cost of $1,000,000. It also cut off the Gulf beaches from the mainland, the resulting area receiving the name of "Pleasure Island."

Electric service came late to Baldwin due to its size and sparse settlement pattern. The distribution of electricity was pioneered by the City of Foley through its Riviera Utilities, which expanded regionally into central and eastern Baldwin. The Baldwin County Electric Co-op, a New Deal REA-sponsored agency, served the remaining portions of the county.

However beneficial the economic programs of the New Deal were to the citizens of Baldwin County, its perceived goals of social and racial leveling were rejected, placing many local Democratic politicians in an untenable position.

Typical was the case of Baldwin's own James (Jimmy) Faulkner, editor of the Baldwin Times. Personally well liked, Faulkner repeatedly tried to patch together his support for the New Deal and his personal political aspirations, but the effort ran into constant roadblocks. One after another of the Democratic leaders of Alabama encountered the same problem with their Baldwin constituents.

In terms of the scope of impact and the long-term changes to life in Baldwin County, World War II produced even greater changes to the fabric of Baldwin County than had the Civil War or World War I. It sent about 2,500 of its sons and daughters to fight, about 60 of that number

Above: Stores in Foley, Alabama.
COURTESY OF THE UNIVERSITY OF SOUTH ALABAMA ARCHIVES.

Below: Commercial corner in Foley, Alabama.
COURTESY OF THE UNIVERSITY OF SOUTH ALABAMA ARCHIVES.

Top: A grocery store interior,
Summerdale, Alabama.
COURTESY OF THE UNIVERSITY OF SOUTH
ALABAMA ARCHIVES.

Above: Flora-Bama Lounge, site of
former outlet of Perdido Bay, Alabama-
Florida state line, Orange Beach.
COURTESY OF BURNETTE PHOTO.

The net effect was a substantial influx of money into the Baldwin economy, and many landowners in the county finally climbed out of debt as a result of the war effort. By 1970 the median family income of Baldwin's population reached $8,000, one of the highest of the non-urban counties in the state. The war years also kicked the population growth into even higher gear, yet the county remained essentially rural in character. County land records indicated a diversification of ownership as a result of the war, with many who had previously lived in rental housing now being able to purchase their own homes.

The political term "liberal" was also a casualty of World War II, and in Alabama it was gradually redefined to mean a "dangerous, reckless, Godless conspiracy to force racial equality upon an unwilling people." When President Truman in 1947 urged the adoption of a civil rights program which included outlawing the poll tax, prohibiting job discrimination on the basis of race, and making lynching a federal offense, that was simply too much for the white voters of Alabama and Baldwin County to stomach. Their own Democratic Party seemed to have delivered a mortal blow which could not be forgiven, and powerful blocks within the Alabama Democratic Party began to bolt. For years more than eighty percent of Baldwin voters had voted the straight Democratic ticket, but in the election of 1948 the county supported the Dixecrat ticket. The transition to Republican Party would be complete in 1950. "Conservative" became a favorite political code word, conveying several levels of meaning, all of them decidedly not "liberal."

Significant industrial development did not take place in the county until after World War II; value added by manufacturing in 1930 in the entire county had been less than $100,000, and that figure was not appreciably higher as late as 1970. These figures do not reflect a shortage of labor or the qualifications of the labor force, but rather the continuing relative isolation of the area. During the same period, cotton production in the county fell from over 125,000 bales to only 20,000, as farmers shifted to less labor-intensive crops. Also in the same period, the black population of the county doubled, and many of them needed jobs which were not available.

The county seat, Bay Minette, became the nexus of industry. There, the Standard Furniture

failing to return, but the lengthened shadow of the conflict has had a continuing effect on the county—socially, politically, and economically.

First, Baldwin was again caught between two important military centers, Mobile as a industrial powerhouse, and Pensacola as a prime military training site. Mobile's war effort was spread over several fields, but shipbuilding was its forte. At the height of the war, approximately 100,000 new workers competed for living space, and that competition spilled over into adjacent Baldwin County. On the east, the Pensacola naval air complex similarly brought thousands of young men into the area, and there was a resulting housing shortage which was only partially satisfied by pressing all available Baldwin shelter into service.

Company provides employment for about 500 workers, producing over 2,500 suites of bedroom furniture each week and giving a continuing market for northern Baldwin hardwood. Kaiser Aluminum produces large-scale high voltage electric cables, while Eastwood-Neally produces fine-mesh woven wire for use in paper mills. Baldwin Pole and Piling Company and International Paper Company's plants draw upon the plentiful supply of pulp and piling wood in the county.

Other commercial activity was scattered about the county. The 'Nut Factory' in Robertsdale, owned by Diamond International, not only processes the tons of nuts grown in the county, but it also imports and packages other

varieties of nuts from all over the world. The Grand Hotel continues to be the largest single employer in the county, while a wholesale nursery in Loxley is perhaps the most beautiful. Oil and natural gas has been found in the Tensaw Delta and offshore near Fort Morgan.

Health care may not be generally thought of as an industry, but in the years following World War II. It has come to be. Foley's first "hospital" was located on the second floor of a drug store at the intersection of routes 98 and 59, but led by Drs. W. C. and Sibley Holmes a new hospital ultimately named the South Baldwin Medical Center replaced it. In Bay Minette the North Baldwin Hospital was built to serve that end of the county.

Massive social change is often an impetus to literary productivity, and the Second World War had such an impact upon Baldwin County. A remarkable group of local authors was moved to prodigious output, drawing upon their observa-

tions of the impact of the war upon the Gulf Coast. Bill Butterworth (writing under the pen name of W. E. B. Griffin) began his monumental serial of praise for the Marine Corps during the war, while Mark Childress chronicled life on the home front in a series of novels which captured the loss of innocence and idealism. Baldwin's very own Fannie Flag came home from college and immediately began writing *Daisy Fay and the Miracle Man*, *Fried Green Tomatoes at the*

❖

Top: Beachfront, Gulf Shores, Alabama.
COURTESY OF THE UNIVERSITY OF SOUTH ALABAMA ARCHIVES.

Middle: A mature pecan orchard, Baldwin County, Alabama.
COURTESY OF BURNETTE PHOTO.

Bottom: Bathers at city pier, Fairhope, Alabama.
COURTESY OF THE UNIVERSITY OF SOUTH ALABAMA ARCHIVES.

Whistle Stop Café, and *Welcome to the World, Baby Girl*, all of which captured the essence of the easy-going lifestyle of the area caught up in modern transition. Fairhope resident Winston Groom reflected a different kind of social realism in his *Better Times Than These*; *As Summers Die*; and *Forrest Gump*, in which he reminded society that its weaker members need special protection. Altogether, it was a remarkable outpouring of literary effort from such a small locale. If nothing else, these authors have given Baldwin County a certain literary cache.

The theme of Baldwin County's development in the last half of the twentieth century was that of promoting itself as a world-class tourist attraction. Somewhat in jest, it has been said that the key to this project was to convince the world that Baldwin was not in Alabama, and it has been crowned with success. The man who

executed this promotional master stroke was George C. Meyer, from St. Paul, Minnesota. Meyer first became familiar with south Baldwin in the 1920s, and he saw development potential where others saw only white sand. Confounding many onlookers, Meyer plunged into acquiring beach property, at one time owning more than 10,000 acres in Gulf Shores. Sales of the property dragged slowly during the Depression, but Meyer bided his time, making many infrastructure improvements at his expense. In a curious capitalization upon fate, Meyer took advantage of several hurricanes as bargain hunters flocked to the Gulf Coast expecting to buy lots at depressed prices. After World War II Meyer had a full-scale land boom on his hands, and other investors and promoters took over where he left off. By the 1960s land was selling by the front-foot, when it had previously been available for a filing fee or a mere pittance on the open market. Baldwin beaches have become the magnet drawing vacationers, "snow birds" (part-time winter residents from northern states), and retirees, each with its own set of perspectives and customs to add new diversity to the county.

The rapid development of Baldwin after the 1960s led inevitably to interest on the part of selected portions of the population for some form of land-use regulation, or zoning. In response, in 1983 the legislature passed an act granting to the County Commission the authority to zone areas south of the Intra-Coastal Waterway and along the Mobile Causeway upon request of the residents and landowners of those areas. That principle of "local option" zoning has subsequently been extended to the entire county.

CHAPTER VII

BALDWIN COUNTY IN THE PRESENT DAY

By the time Baldwin County celebrated its 200th birthday, it had changed radically from a frontier community on the remote Gulf Coast to a vibrant, rapidly developing area which had been only recently been "discovered" by the outside world. Its development and economic expansion continues at an accelerating pace.

The population of Baldwin County in 2000 had grown to 140,415, in 55,336 households, representing an increase from 98,280 just ten years earlier. The annual increase is estimated at 3.8 per cent, compared with the state of Alabama at 0.4 per cent per year. Baldwin's growth for the ten years prior to 2000 was 42.9 per cent, second only in Alabama to Shelby County, which includes the southern suburbs of Birmingham.

Baldwin's recent rapid growth has been due to two principal factors: retirees discovering the attractions of the area and the growth of a substantial commuting population to jobs outside the county. In 1990 there were 13,339 out-commuters in the county compared with 3,096 in-commuters, but by the census of 2000 both figures had increased sharply. The resulting settlement pattern has resulted in a concentration of growth on the maritime fringe, along the Eastern Shore, the Gulf beach area, and Perdido Bay. That pattern may be expected to continue.

The massive influx of retirees has skewed the normal demographic distribution of the population. In 2000 persons under age five accounted for 6.1 per cent of the population, compared with 6.7 per cent in the state at large. School-age children, 6-18, made up 24.4 per cent of the population, compared to 25.3 per cent in Alabama at large. Persons over the age of 65 comprised 15.5 per cent of the population, with the Alabama portion being 13.0 per cent. Baldwin residents with a college education made up 23.1 per cent of the total, while that group in Alabama amounted to 19.0 percent.

Baldwin's people are about as widely dispersed but economically better off than Alabama's population; the Baldwin density is 88.0 per square mile compared to 87.6 in Alabama. The median value of Baldwin owner-occupied housing units is $122,500 and the median household income is $40,250, while the comparable figures for the state as a whole is $85,100 for home values and $34,135 for household income.

Economic activity in Baldwin has tended steadily from farming and ranching to a myriad of service enterprises generally associated with the growth of the retired population and tourism. In 1999 there

Alabama Pass, Orange Beach, Alabama.
COURTESY OF BURNETTE PHOTO.

were 3,837 operating farms employing 42,848 persons, representing an 83.4 percent decline over the previous decade. The new and expanding economic activity leans heavily towards retail trade and services. Retail trade is the largest single sector, with 801 units employing 7,850. Annual payroll is $114,784,000, and annual sales are $1,215,305,000. The second-largest sector is public accommodation and food services. A total of 303 units employ 6,337, with an annual payroll of $61,034,000.

Health care represents the third-largest sector and the most rapidly growing, with 222 units employing 1,901, and an annual payroll of $51,821,000. Annual income of $105,539,000 makes it the growth industry in the county.

Closely following is professional and technical services, with 225 units employing 918, annual payroll of $29,200,000, and gross sales of $69,562,000. Real estate sales and rentals were served by 195 units employing 1,139, with an annual payroll of $19,569,000, and a gross income of $81,759,000. Manufacturing was at the bottom of the leading economic activities, with 138 units employing 5,150, annual payroll of $127,054,000, and gross production of $809,523,000.

Baldwin's greatest attraction in its recent dizzy development also continues to be its nemesis, and the fact was driven home during the night of September 15-16, 2004, when Hurricane Ivan ("The Terrible") roared ashore at Gulf Shores. Easily the most destructive storm to visit the Gulf Coast in years, the water surge of up to 25 feet and winds of up to 130 miles per hour wreaked havoc on property. Only mandatory evacuation prevented extensive loss of life. Property losses ran to the billions of dollars, but hearty developers saw new opportunities in replacing damaged or destroyed single-family cottages with high-rise condos. Nothing seems to brake the onward rush of development save running out of land on which to build.

As Baldwin confidently rushes forward to fulfill its destiny, it continues to display many of the same characteristics which have set it apart since the earliest days of its remarkable history. Wilderness lies less than ten miles distant from the teeming vacation shore of the Gulf. It remains fiercely independent, even populist in spirit. A land of economic opportunity, it places high value on the quiet life style of earlier years. A world unto itself, its maritime and isolated location has often thrust it onto the stage of important, even international events. It has assimilated immigrants from a wide variety of places and backgrounds and melded their progeny into a remarkably homogeneous society. It warmly welcomes newcomers, yet it expects them to leave behind invidious comparisons with their origins. The result is a distinctive, if not unique, coastal paradise—not always comfortable with its own success, and never certain of its relationship with the rest of Alabama. It is a place where one is not easily bored, where retirement is a joy, and where untold opportunity lies around every bend. Steeped in a storied past, it rushes forward to claim its future—whatever that may be.

Note: Readers who desire a more detailed and documented treatment of the same subject are referred to the author's study, Coastal Kingdom: A History of Baldwin County, Alabama (Frederick, Maryland: Publish America, 2006)

The intersection at 59 and 98 in Foley, Alabama.

COURTESY OF ALABAMA TOURISM & TRAVEL AND DAN BROTHERS

COURTESY OF ALABAMA TOURISM & TRAVEL AND DAN BROTHERS

COURTESY OF ALABAMA TOURISM & TRAVEL AND KARIM SHAMSI-BASHA

COURTESY OF MAURENE SEAQUIST.

COURTESY OF NORTH BALDWIN CHAMBER OF COMMERCE

COURTESY OF JUDY BADONSKY.

COURTESY OF EASTERN SHORE CHAMBER OF COMMERCE.

COURTESY OF EASTERN SHORE CHAMBER OF COMMERCE.

SHARING THE HERITAGE

historic profiles of businesses,

organizations, and families that have

contributed to the development

and economic base of Baldwin County

SPECIAL THANKS TO

DeSoto's

Dyer Package Store

Gulf Shores Rentals

Hotel Magnolia

Littledudeartwork.com

Microtel Inn -
Souvenir City

Moore Bros.
Village Market &
Jesse's Restaurant

ONO Professional
Partners

Sylvan Learning Center

MALBIS PLANTATION

The names of visionary early pioneers such as Jason Malbis are synonymous with the historic legacy that stretches across a century of life in Baldwin County. Today, that legacy remains at the heart of Malbis Plantation, Inc., a successful land holding and real estate development company. Its history is as unique and exciting as any in southern Alabama.

Malbis was first settled by Greek immigrants in 1906, while Malbis Plantation was eventually incorporated in February 1933. Yet it all began with a poor young man who was taken by his father from Dournena, Greece, the place of his birth in 1866, to the nearby monastery of the Great Cave (Mega Spilaion) in order to be educated there and hear the word of God.

The young man, whose name was Antonios Markopoulos, remained in the monastery for several years humbly performing the duties of a monk

Jason Malbis, 1908.

and diligently observing the teachings of the Gospel. The teachings of the Gospel became his companion for life. However, the narrow confines of the monastery were too confining for an active and ambitious young man, who wanted to live his life assisting his fellow man especially along Christian, humanitarian and philanthropic lines. In the early part of the last century, young poor people from Greece immigrated to the United States by the thousands, in pursuit of the good things in life.

Antonios felt it an opportune time to follow many of his compatriots, so that he might teach them to apply Christian principles to their every day lives. He finally landed in America and settled himself in Chicago, where he applied for and legally changed his name to Jason Malbis.

In 1906, he and a friend, William Papageorge, set out in search of the land of their

dreams. They traveled the country working in various cities in Illinois, Missouri, Oklahoma, Texas, and Mississippi until one day they found themselves in Mobile, Alabama.

Their meager finances had dwindled and they were exhausted and despaired. Of all the property they had seen, none was suitable for their intended purposes. So they decided to extend their stay in Mobile to obtain employment and replenish their funds and to rest for a few weeks. Late one afternoon they were sitting on a bench in Bienville Square discussing the Gospel and were reminded of the scripture: "The earth is the Lord's and the fullness thereof." At that moment they spotted a poster in a window of a nearby building that advertised "Low Cost Farmlands for Sale."

Their English was as poor as they were and they relied on their English-Greek dictionary to

Malbis Bakery, 1945.

translate the poster's inscription. They contacted the realtor, Weafel, the following day and purchased 250 acres for $6.00 per acre to establish the Greek settlement, a high price for land in those days without water frontage. The property was undeveloped and the immigrants worked in many forms of unpleasant conditions to develop what is now Malbis Plantation, Inc. It was necessary for the immigrants to build and manage their own electric company, ice plant, nursery, and to farm the land in order to survive without the modern conveniences that we are blessed with today.

After Malbis and Papageorge plowed through the tangled underbrush for hours with the real estate dealer from Mobile, they came to the same conclusion. They would not buy the land. As they were returning to the boat, which brought them across the bay to see the land, Malbis stopped. As he shared the experience later, he described a bright light shining in the sky, felt a hand on his shoulder, and heard a voice from nowhere saying: "This is the place."

After making a meager down payment on the land and making a note for the rest, they took their last $25.00 and purchased axes, dynamite, grubbing hoes, and seed potatoes. They slept on the floor of an abandoned shack in the woods while they dug and blasted out stumps, cleared the brush, and planted the seed potatoes. They harvested a good crop in the spring as a result of the sandy soil of South Alabama being a great producer of potatoes.

With potato money, Malbis went to Chicago to recruit more help. John Vocolis was an early settler at Malbis. He had knowledge of medicine and when more Greeks came, he would doctor them. He also treated sick horses and cows successfully. His greatest contribution was a little one-oven bakery that he built for use of the colony. The popularity of his baked bread soon spread throughout the surrounding countryside. Baldwin County in those days was full of hopeful colonies of foreigners Frenchman, Italians, Scandinavians, Germans, and Bohemians, those who remembered from childhood the great taste of homemade breads, began to buy bread from the Greeks.

This fit Malbis' intention to establish a working colony that would grow and prosper by providing things that were needed in the community. He purchased a small bakery in Fairhope and began to bake bread for the Eastern Shore.

At one time, Malbis Plantation was 10,000 acres with a population of 75. The property ranged from the bluff of Lake Forest for four miles along what is today Interstate 10, Timber Creek, the Eastern Shore Centre and schools from Daphne High School to Rockwell Elementary School. The crowning achieve-ment is the Malbis Memorial Church built in 1965 made of stone from Greece and hand painted frescos of gold leaf. The Byzantine inspired architecture is one of the finest examples in the United States. Also, Malbis Memorial Foundation was established to perpetuate the church properties and support local charities.

Jason Malbis, 1930.

The Malbis Plantation had its own bakery, dairy and community with dorms for men and women. The bakery was located in downtown Mobile and thrived as did many other Malbis Plantation businesses including restaurants and a motel. Still the community continues under generations of leadership after Malbis' death, selling land to Diamondhead Corporation to create Lake Forest; Alabama's largest subdivision. Antigone Papageorge was president during the 1970s when land was sold for the exclusive Timber Creek golf development. She also donated land for a park of giant oak trees, today known as Centennial Park.

In 1997 when George Malbis became the next president, Historic Malbis residential and commercial development and the

Eastern Shore Centre, a regional lifestyle center on Interstate 10 were developed. Today the shareholders consist of Maria Athanasios, Antonia Cleondis, Alexandra Doussa, Eugenia Eftaxa, George Kalasountas, Gertrude Malbis, Thomas G. Malbis, George Mathews, Bessie Papas, Despina Pappas, Nick Rapanos, George Scourtes, William J. Scourtes, Harry Stavrakos, James Stavrakos, Nick Stavrakos, Paul Stavrakos, Nick Tsaltas, and James Wilkinson.

A century of progress has not dimmed that pioneer spirit that led Malbis to follow his dreams and create a life for him and others that has honored the great reverence he had for the rich land around him.

Today, Malbis Plantation's primary mission is to aggressively manage its assets as to enhance value as a long term investment for the Plantation shareholders, and to increase its value for those who reside and work

Malbis Plantation
Daphne, Ala.

in the area. They believe that a conscientious, planned and practical supervision of the Plantation properties is a sensible investment strategy, both in economic terms and of preserving the quality of life of the area in which the land is situated.

Malbis Plantation's reverence for the land and the vision of their founders causes each one to recognize that key portions of this land should remain as it was inherited, well preserved and, where appropriate, improved for future age groups. In this sense the case for historical or conservation will always be given equal position to contending property uses.

Malbis Plantation was established with core Christian principles as its main source of guidance. In all things, they are determined to conduct their affairs honestly, reasonably and morally; and are prepared to assign a reasonable share of the rewards and success where they will help address problems of the county that extend outside the property and of their direct self-interest.

Today land continues to be the major asset and developing land happens only rarely as time and the real estate market dictates. The generations have dwindled over time, but the vision remains with the latest President William J. Scourtes. His hope on the one-hundredth birthday of Malbis Plantation and the bicentennial of Baldwin County is to preserve the remarkable past history and to tell its story of immigration, spiritual journeys, commerce and American ingenuity in the heart of Alabama's fastest growing county—Baldwin County.

In memory of: William Papageorge, Chris C. Papageorge, Chrysanthe Papageorge, Fotene Chris Papageorge, Marie Jane Starkey, John Vogalis, Philip Papas, Efstratios E. Papas, Stamatra Papas, George E. Papas, James E. Papas, Gus E. Papas, Fotene Papas, Antigone Papageorge, Marie Jane Starkey, Nafseka J. Mallars, Nicholas C. Stadrakos, Eflhemias P. Vrahatis, James Mallars, Helen Kokenes Mallars, Themistokles C, Kokenes, Evangelos Karamanos, Perry N. Kontopoulos, Nicholaos Kontopoulos, Olympia Kontopoulos, Panayiota John Kinnas, Dr. George C. Papageorge, Tula Petrinou Papageorge, Fred Peter Gregor, Lora Cometti Gregor, Emmanuel S. Larnbrakis, Peter Gregor, Efstratios W. Kontopoulos, Sofia E. Kontopoulos, Constantine Papadeas, Frankos Peter Epaminouda, Panayiote Athanasios Malbis, Harry Andrews, James Dardamis, Constantine G. Staurojohn, Stergios Zigo Gouletsas, George M. Peturis, Pauline N. Kospetos, John A. Mercouris, Paulline N. Kospetos, John A. Mercouris, Thomas G. Mathews, Angela Mathews, James J. Mathews, Christina G. Mathews, John F. Anargyros, Athanasios Anargyros, Chris Anargyros, Theodore N. Hangis, Minnie Marina Marinos, George Demetriou Marinos, Mimis Chapralis, George J. Frankos, Nicolaos P. Kontupoulos, Alexious Tragos, Epaminondas Papas, Perioles Kontojohn, John Efthemios Hanjes, Anthony Farmakis, Nell George Kalasountas, Leimonia "Lula" Papas, Athanasia G. Papas, Sam G. Papas, John George Peturis, George Peter Malbis, Mark Edward Malbis, Constantinos Scourtes, Mary Gregor Wilkinson, Harry Peter Gregor, Julia A. Gregor, Anthony P. and Antigone Betsiaras, Constantine Tampary and Alexandra M. Tampary.

Malbis Plantation Home, 1930.

WADE WARD REAL ESTATE, INC.

George Charles Meyer was a quiet, thoughtful, tenacious, and thoroughly optimistic man who had a clear and unshakable vision of Gulf Shores, years before it became a reality.

Such men are called prophets. George probably would have scoffed at that notion. "He was an unassuming man," according to his widow, the late Erie Hall Meyer. Wade Ward, president of The George C. Meyer Foundation and Wade Ward Real Estate, says, "He was a dreamer who was also a very practical man. He lived in the real world—make no mistake about it."

Born the son of immigrant German parents in New Prague, Minnesota, in 1878, George lived a storybook life that included making and losing several fortunes in real estate. He was fortunate to have met and exchanged ideas with men like Carl Graham Fisher, who developed Miami Beach. These meetings with others of like mind helped him to pursue his burning ambitions of a magnificent world-class all-seasons resort in the white southern tip of his beloved adopted state on the warm waters of the Gulf of Mexico.

Gulf Shores was his creation. He built it from his own dreams and, to a great extent, with his own hands. He discovered this thirty-two-mile paradise of powdery white beaches, warm blue Gulf, inland lakes, and gentle breezes long before anyone even knew it existed. And, his vision took shape. It never diminished.

"The word 'can't' was not in his vocabulary," said Erie. "He simply never doubted his own intuition. I don't think it ever occurred to him that Gulf Shores wouldn't someday become what he knew it would become—one of the most beautiful resorts in the world."

He came to Alabama in 1921 at the age of forty-two. He had prospered in land speculation and the abstract business in Michigan and Washington. Meanwhile, his love of tennis was bearing fruit. He played the circuit of the eastern coast and won the Georgia State Tennis Championship. While in Florida, where he enjoyed playing all winter on inside courts, he met and became friends with another dreamer and doer, Carl Graham Fisher. The two talked, swapped ideas, shared dreams of golden resorts that one day would rival the famous spas and playgrounds of Europe and the Mediterranean.

Inspired, George toured the lush but barren coastal areas of Florida, pushed westward to Pensacola, and from there into the nearly uninhabited region of Alabama. "He was struck by the beauty and the tropical climate of this area," Erie said, "and by the realization that in the entire State of Alabama, there are only thirty-two miles of Gulf front. He knew that, sooner or later, that stretch of territory would be valuable."

He visited Mobile and was immediately charmed by the city—one of the oldest in America, and in many ways a culture that mixed the Old World gentility and New World spirit of fun and frivolity and adventure. He lived at the famous old Battle House Hotel in Mobile and was thoroughly captured by the beauty and graciousness of the South, so he adopted the South as his homeland for the rest of his life.

George purchased ten thousand acres of land in Alabama, all of it undeveloped, all of it in Baldwin County near the Gulf of Mexico, the part of the state that had first lured him from Florida. But the area which interested him most was still little more than swamp and wilderness, unowned, uninhabited and considered almost uninhabitable by the government. It was without roads, communications, still practically unexplored since the days of the first Spanish adventure in the area in 1519. In those days, in the 1920s, the government was trying to encourage settlement there, so homesteading was encouraged. That was just the kind adventure that appealed to George. If someone was interested in homesteading the process was to pay $50 down, build a cabin or cottage and live in it a required number of days and nights of the year. After one proved he had stayed the required period of time, he paid a final amount and the land was his. Erie said he went homesteading with a love and a vengeance. He loved wildlife, birds, the native growth here, the wildness and solitude. And all the time he had his vision that, someday, all this would be a beautiful, carefully developed, enchanting place for people to live and vacation and bring their families.

Erie remarked that, "George could sit on the front porch of our home and look out and remember days when he had faced long stretches of solitude in little more than a shack, dreaming and working, and to know that that dream had come true. He could almost hold it in his hand. Maybe that's why he never doubted that his other, larger dreams of Gulf Shores resort, would come true as well."

Disaster struck George in 1928. The stock market crash and Depression, which wiped out so many dreams for so many people, put an end to this way of life for George. While on a visit to Europe, he learned that economic collapse in the United States had left him practically penniless, but the beloved land was yet his. He picked up the pieces and started all over again. He controlled quite a bit of land but there was very little money. He still dreamed of developing the area on the Gulf Coast and even in the blackest moments of those times believed that it would become a reality. But he had a hard time convincing anybody else.

George made many trips to the state legislature in those bleak days following the Depression to talk to anyone who would listen. He offered the state thousands of acres of his holdings as a donation for the site of a state park. Part of which is now Gulf State Park, the most successful state park facility in Alabama today, containing three lakes and 6,000 acres, heavily utilized by the public and returning a good investment, started as a gift from this remarkable man.

Determined to see his dream become a reality and discovering that no one else was interested in it, or believed it possible, George realized he would have to build the dream with his own imagination and muscle.

Using what money and resources he could muster, he settled on the finger of land (now an island, severed from the mainland by creation of the Intracoastal Waterway) which he called "Gulf Shores," built a hotel, designed, engineered, and actually helped build roads and highways and bridges that would lead to habitation and visitation from the outside world. It was not easy.

For the first eight years, he could not sell a single piece of land. Nobody cared. He continued to talk, to dream, to work. He donated land with no strings attached to the small community that was beginning to take shape on the island. George, Erie and Ward later donated land for parks, a golf course, a track of land sufficiently large enough for an elementary, middle and a high school; land for the municipal and community buildings, including the Civic Center and Faulkner Community College and also gulf frontage for the Gulf Shores Public Beach; and all thirteen churches were gifted with part or all of their land for sanctuaries. At today's prices, the donations would be in excess of $500 million.

George Charles Meyer.

When George died in 1959 at the age of eighty, Gulf Shores had been incorporated for only three years, but the dream was launched.

George created the Meyer Foundation before his death, to continue, by generous donations of lands and interest, his dream. When Hurricane Frederic struck and devastated the beaches and much of the city in 1979, it was the privilege of the Meyer entities to work with the town, churches and government bodies to help lift the island back to its feet.

The tourist boom in Alabama, in the South, in the nation, hit full stride in the early 1970s, and suddenly Gulf Shores became the focal point of tremendous interest by developers. Private interests realized the potential of the sun and sand and access to the Gulf of Mexico, the close proximity to Florida on the one side and New Orleans on the other, the mammoth potential market of Mobile, the fact the Interstate 65 created a clear corridor from Wisconsin, Michigan, and Canada, directly to Gulf Shores. The federal government made funds available for recovery operations from the hurricane; the state took a sudden interest in the area as a magnet for tourist dollars to boost the Alabama economy.

Suddenly, the vision that George had held almost alone for nearly sixty years was about to happen. If only he could have been there to witness it.

In 1960, his nephew, Wade Ward, took up the gauntlet that George had lain down, perpetuating the legacy that his uncle had begun. Ward worked hard to contribute to the development of Alabama's "pearl of the gulf" without destroying the very qualities that had drawn people to the area to begin with.

In the early 1970s, Ward and his partner, Claude O'Connor, created Meyer Real Estate. Although "Meyer" was used in the name of the company, there was never any ownership of the Meyer family then or today. Later, Ward sold his interest to his partner and created Wade Ward Real Estate.

Ward worked tirelessly to help build Gulf Shores into the astonishing destination that it is today. But he balanced that with an eye toward preserving the integrity of an economy where families live, work, and play, a place where people travel from hundreds of miles away to experience a wholesome, peaceful lifestyle that uniquely defines Gulf Shores.

Ward has developed more than thirty-nine subdivisions in the area. The company also has invested its proceeds in the community and Ward has a Nature Park and the Campus of Faulkner State Community College named for him.

In recent years, a third generation has joined the cause. All four of the Ward children have worked in the business and share the creative genius, idealism, and determination first displayed by their great-uncle, George Meyer, and has taken up the community-building banner. This philosophy is evident in the company's "small-by-design" business methodology that focuses on one-on-one relationships with its customers and in its inherent desire to serve, give, and help.

In an era when impersonal ambition often takes precedence over genuine service, Wade Ward Real Estate takes pride in the accomplishments of a determined family eager to share the wonder of Gulf Shores. While other real estate companies concentrate on the numbers, the family at Wade Ward Real Estate renders caring, conscientious, old-fashioned service.

The Ward family believes Gulf Shores is more than a place to live, it is a lifestyle. Those who yearn to partake in the area's marvelous lifestyle deserve to be greeted warmly and receive top-notch service from Gulf Shores' most noteworthy ambassadors. Let the staff at Wade Ward Real Estate devote its time to making you completely satisfied with your purchase of an existing condo, home, or commercial property. The staff can also help locate the perfect spot for a new home, condo, or business, or call on Wade Ward Real Estate to help you plan your future with a site for a future home.

Nearly a century has passed since an idealistic and eager young man discovered a passion for living in Gulf Shores and sought to share it with others.

Wade Ward Real Estate has built upon George's dream to create a legacy of its own. With almost five decades of experience on the Alabama coast, it is easy to see that the Ward family is committed to the area.

❖

Wade Ward.

Founded in 1979 as the Baldwin County Humane Society, the Baldwin Animal Rescue Center was organized by a group of citizens concerned about inadequate animal control and animal cruelty ordinances and the lack of a professional approach to dealing with stray, abused and abandoned animals. At that time, there were no animal shelters in Baldwin County and stray animals were dispatched by gunshot.

This group, led by Maria Wynne Gwynn, convinced public officials to construct a county animal shelter. Over time, the more progressive communities hired animal control officers and constructed municipal shelters. State legislators were encouraged to enact changes in Alabama's animal cruelty statutes.

Today the Baldwin Animal Rescue Center (B.A.R.C.) offers adoption and rescue services to all residents of Baldwin County. B.A.R.C. provides comprehensive low cost spay/neuter programs with options for low income families and individuals receiving Medicaid. Services are also available to families dealing with illness, death of a family member or military obligation.

B.A.R.C. is the lead agency for the Maddie's Fund Pet Rescue project in Baldwin County. This coalition of animal rescue and animal control organizations is dedicated to eliminating the euthanization of stray and abandoned animals. To achieve this goal pet adoptions are held at high-profile, high-traffic locations throughout Baldwin County. Matching the right animal with the right family, B.A.R.C. has placed over ten thousand dogs and cats in new homes since 1998.

The rapid growth of Baldwin County has resulted in an increased number of stray and abandoned dogs and cats, straining the resources of rescue and animal control agencies. B.A.R.C. believes that spaying or neutering pets is an important step in reducing the number of stray and abandoned animals. In addition to preventing the birth of unwanted puppies and kittens, spayed and neutered animals tend to be healthier and happier, and live longer.

B.A.R.C. is located at 306 Magnolia Avenue in Fairhope. For additional information, please visit www.baldwinanimalrescue.com.

UNIVERSITY OF SOUTH ALABAMA BALDWIN COUNTY

In 1984 the University of South Alabama established a branch campus in Baldwin County. It was created to offer partial degree programs with upper-level undergraduate courses (junior and senior level) and graduate courses. The first classes met in September 1984 on the campus of Faulkner State Junior College in Bay Minette with fewer than one hundred students.

The University of South Alabama Baldwin County (USABC) began offering courses in Fairhope in 1986 to meet the demands of population growth in the southern part of the county. Since the beginning, enrollment at USABC has grown steadily. The curriculum has expanded and now students who have completed the University's general education requirements can complete undergraduate degrees at USABC. Graduate degrees are also offered.

In 1998 the administration at the University changed and a renewed commitment was made to meet the higher education needs of one of the fastest growing areas in the state. Beginning college students can meet their general education

requirements by taking lower division courses (freshman and sophomore level) at the University of South Alabama's main campus and complete their degrees at USABC. Students may transfer course credits from accredited higher education institutions located throughout the United States and complete their degrees at USABC.

Dr. Phillip Norris, director of USABC, says of the opportunities available at the site, "We pride ourselves on our quick administrative response to students' needs. By scheduling timely courses we work to provide quality education that is both useful and accessible to meet the needs of full-time, part-time and non-traditional students alike."

Bachelor's degrees at USABC include the Adult Degree Program, business administration, public relations in communication, criminal justice, elementary education, and nursing, which offers both a traditional and accelerated track. A minor in psychology is offered.

❖

Above: The Performance Center.

Below: A classroom complex.

Many outstanding and unique activities that go beyond the classroom are available on the campus of USABC. The Performance Center is used for community events throughout the year. The Fairhope Film Festival is held on the campus and is sponsored by USABC, the M. W. Smith, Jr. Foundation, and the Alabama State Council on the Arts. It is open to anyone in the community and offers films not usually shown in area commercial movie theaters.

USABC and Baldwin County United created and sponsor Leadership Baldwin County. It is a countywide program to enhance leadership skills and meets monthly from October through May every other year. Adults who live in the county are encouraged to apply for the program.

The Baldwin County branch of University of South Alabama is located in Fairhope on the beautiful Eastern Shore of Mobile Bay and its informative website can be found at www.southalabama.edu/usabc.

❖

Left: The Administration Building.

Below: A USABC classroom.

Master's degree programs include elementary education, educational administration, counseling, and special education (collaborative). Courses are generally held once weekly in the evenings, which makes classes convenient for students who work during the day. Degree programs are also offered during the day. Online courses are available as scheduled by the academic departments. Once admitted, students can register for courses offered at any University location.

Practicum, clinical course work, and internship requirements in areas such as education and nursing may be met in healthcare and education facilities located in Baldwin County and the surrounding areas. Courses in business, education, and liberal arts are offered each semester that can be used as elective credits in a variety of degree programs.

GRAND HOTEL MARRIOTT RESORT, GOLF CLUB & SPA

Experience a stunning Alabama beach resort at the exquisite Grand Hotel Marriott Resort, Golf Club and Spa. Situated on 550 secluded, waterfront acres in Point Clear, this Alabama resort features a rich history dating back to 1847. Offering a dramatic departure from southern resorts, The Grand Hotel boasts two challenging golf courses as part of the Robert Trent Jones Golf Trail, as well as a luxurious 20,000 square foot European-style spa, a fabulous array of exceptional dining options, and a sizeable marina for sailboats, yachts, and fishing boats.

The delightful beaches and extraordinary pool complex offer plenty of entertainment for the whole family. Overlooking scenic Mobile Bay, this Gulf Coast resort boasts 37,000 square feet of elegant meeting and event space for corporate events that defy convention, and weddings that dreams are made of. Escape from ordinary beach resorts and discover The Grand Hotel, the Queen of Southern Resorts.

The Grand has five buildings containing 405 beautiful rooms and thirty-six suites, providing a refreshing alternative to most accommodations. The hotel also has

The Room That Works® guest rooms. Guests enjoy lavish comforts, including the new Revive® bedding package from Marriott as well as spacious, newly renovated hotel rooms that boast generous proportions and added amenities. Many rooms offer beautiful views of the bay or marina while others provide pool and garden vistas. Guests can experience an abundance of family friendly amenities at this stunning, historic, beachfront resort.

The Grand Hotel houses seven different restaurants and lounges to complete the resort experience. Open for breakfast and lunch, The Dining Room serves American food, offering exquisite breakfast buffets,

tasty lunches, and Award Winning Sunday Brunches. The Lakewood Club and Grill Room allows guests to celebrate a great round of golf or a gathering of friends and family. Sample a great offering of sandwiches and other daily chef offerings for lunch, featuring fresh local ingredients. The Grand Dining Room is the resort's upscale-casual dining environment featuring bold wines, crisp, farm fresh produce and hand-

picked herbs from the Chef's Herb Garden and great steaks and seafood. Bucky's Birdcage Lounge provides a place for friends to kick back for a light meal or drinks with live entertainment nightly. The Pelican's Nest and Marlin Bar are two seasonal poolside locations serving cool drinks, grilled favorites, sandwiches and snacks during the lunch and dinner hours. The Grand Coffee Shop is open for breakfast and lunch and invites you to start your day with a latte or the signature "Grand Hotel Special" accompanied by a pastry shop-made biscotti or freshly baked delights from the Pastry Shoppe. The Saltwater Grill is an amazing, upbeat, unique, casual and entertaining atmosphere serving dinner choices such as fresh, local seafood.

Recreation opportunities abound at The Grand Hotel. Whether a guest pines for

swimming, biking, jet-skiing, jogging/fitness trail, kayaking, sailing, tennis, croquet, horseshoes, volleyball, golf, or simply relaxing at the spa—this resort has it! If offsite adventure is more what a guest has in mind, several attractions and landmarks are within driving distance to suit every fancy. Whether it is visiting the *USS Alabama* Battleship, Pensacola Naval Air Museum, the Gulf Coast Exploreum and IMAX, Fort Conde, the Bragg-Mitchell Mansion, or the Bellingath Garden & Home, a guest is sure to be entertained. Boundless shopping opportunities are available, as well, from small downtown-style shopping in Fairhope to the Tanger Center Outlet Mall.

For more information, visit the Grand Hotel Marriott Resort Golf Club & Spa on the Internet at www.marriottgrand.com.

BALDWIN COUNTY ELECTRIC MEMBERSHIP CORPORATION

The member-owned Baldwin County Electric Membership Corporation (Baldwin EMC) is a customer-focused, efficient and community-involved cooperative that distributes electricity to its members and provides street lighting and surge protection devices.

Founded on April 22, 1937, Baldwin EMC was incorporated by Frank Earle of Blacksher, P.A. Bryant of Stockton, Alton Hankins of Robertsdale, Frank Hoffman of Elberta, and Tom Steele, Jr., of Bon Secour, who also served as the corporation's first directors.

When the corporation converted to a cooperative in 1939, it was divided into districts, for which the first trustees were Frank Earle, District 1, president; Alton Hankins, District 2; Ed Kane, District 3, secretary; Frank Hoffman, District 4; and Tom Steele Jr., District 5.

A branch office was opened in Gulf Shores in 1968, and Baldwin EMC moved into a new complex in Summerdale in 1972, which still serves as its headquarters. A branch office opened in Bay Minette in 1974 and the Monroe County warehouse/field office opened in 1995.

After Hurricane Frederic destroyed many of the existing structures along the beaches of Gulf Shores and Orange Beach in September 1979, the resulting building boom was significant in development of the area. The coastal area's development has sparked tremendous economic growth, primarily in tourism.

Baldwin EMC, which is the sole electrical provider for the coastal area of the county, has been a leader in technological advances. It was the first utility in the county to implement twenty-four-hour manned dispatch services, tremendously improving response time and improving customer satisfaction. The System Control and Data Acquisition system installed in 1989 gives Baldwin EMC state-of-the-art control over its electrical distribution system and minimizes outage time. A fully staffed control center was established in 1995 with four full-time dispatchers, trained to operate SCADA and PORCHE (automated outage reporting system).

In 1998, Baldwin EMC joined Touchstone Energy, a national alliance of local, member-owned electric cooperatives that do business with integrity, accountability, innovation and commitment to community. Touchstone Energy provides the resources of a nationwide network to bring added value and benefit to Baldwin EMC's customers, while emphasizing the importance of its local presence and unique ties to the community.

Establishment of the Baldwin Electric Membership Charitable Foundation in 2004 allows the cooperative to round up participating members' bills to the next dollar. The extra cents from each bill are collected and placed in the Foundation for redistribution to meet needs in the Baldwin County area. These funds are granted for food, clothing, healthcare, shelter, education, and the environment. Since distribution began in 2004, more than

$480,000 has been granted to local organizations and individuals.

Baldwin EMC distributes power over 4,062.6 miles of line, in a service area that covers most of Baldwin County and a section of southern Monroe County. It serves two of the twelve municipalities and most of the unincorporated areas of Baldwin County. The Co-op's statistics for 2005 show 179 employees; $93,210,991 in revenue; $3,251,147 in margins/net income; and $68,791,794 in equity/net worth.

The availability of reliable electricity is critical to economic development, so the presence of Baldwin EMC has been vital to development of this county. The strongest evidence is to be seen along the Alabama Gulf Coast, which is now a high-profile resort area. Without reliable electric service, none of this development would be possible.

Deeply involved in community and charitable activities, Baldwin EMC is a member of all five chambers of commerce in Baldwin County, the Business Council of Alabama, and the Alabama Home Builders Association.

Employees are members of many organizations, including Rotary and Kiwanis clubs, and serve on the boards of the Home

Builders Association, chambers of commerce, Baldwin County Economic Development Alliance, Public Transportation Coalition, and *USS Alabama* Battleship Commission.

In addition, Baldwin EMC sponsors numerous local charities and events, and its employees are involved in many community organizations, from volunteer fire departments to PTA groups, youth and adult ball teams, and religious groups.

KAISER REALTY, INCORPORATED

Leonard A. Kaiser stared at the devastation wrought by Hurricane Fredrick on the Alabama coast in 1979 and saw opportunity in the barren sand where his and other homes had once stood.

So, in January 1980, Kaiser opened Kaiser Realty, Inc. to help turn Alabama's thirty-two mile-long coastline into a vacation destination and home to people yearning to live by the sea.

Today, Kaiser Realty, Inc., is a leader in Gulf Coast vacation rentals, real estate sales and property management services. Beginning with a handful of properties in 1980, Kaiser's portfolio of properties has grown to more than seven hundred and the company is now a multifaceted company specializing in vacation rentals, real estate sales, property management and association management services.

For a long time, most people did not even know Alabama had a beach. They know now, thanks to Kaiser and others in the Gulf Shores/Orange Beach area. The small resort community has grown from a relatively unknown, seasonal vacation spot to a thriving year-round vacation destination.

The company has grown because of its commitment to providing the absolute best service to owners, guests and real estate customers. Kaiser has grown the company in a controlled, targeted direction with the focus on quality rather than quantity. The company developed a tradition of fulfilling dreams for customers, employees and the community by delivering exceptional, professional service with integrity, enthusiasm and genuine caring attitude. Whether it's for a vacation or a lifetime, the Kaiser Realty family is committed to helping the families that visit and live here.

The company's success is due in great part to its dedicated employees. Many have been with the company for fifteen years or more and two have retired from the company with fifteen-plus years of service. The company's number one source of reservations is repeat guests, reflecting the company's commitment to providing quality service.

Kaiser Realty was chosen as the association management company for Summer House on Romar Beach Condominiums, one of the area's first upscale condominium developments projects, a property it continues to service today. The company has offices in Gulf Shores, Orange Beach and an on-site office at Summer House on Romar Beach. Kaiser Realty began construction on a new office in Gulf Shores in January 2006.

Other complexes managed by Kaiser Realty include Admirals Quarters

twenty-fifth anniversary in 2005, a unique accomplishment in the dynamic coastal community.

Through active participation and serving in leadership positions with the Alabama Gulf Coast Area Chamber of Commerce and the Alabama Gulf Coast Area Convention and Visitors Bureau, the company has played a vital role in directing the tourism growth of the area.

The company, its founder and employees are committed to giving back to the community. Kaiser Realty is recognized for its leadership in and dedication to supporting area schools, churches and charitable organizations. The company also has given substantial support to national humanitarian organizations, including the American Heart Association, the American Cancer Society and the South Baldwin County United Way. In 2001, Leonard A. Kaiser received the first Distinguished Service Award by the Alabama Gulf Coast Area Chamber of Commerce.

Fulfilling dreams is part of the way Kaiser Realty does business, and will continue to be a motivating force behind its business and its commitment to the Gulf Shores/Orange Beach community.

Condominiums, Beachside Romar Homes, The Enclave Condominiums, The Palms Condominiums, Palm Harbor Condominiums, Tidewater Condominiums and Crystal Shores Condominiums.

The company was instrumental in developing the Vacation Rental Manager's Association, the first national association to address the unique aspects of property management and vacation rentals. Kaiser Realty is the first rental management company to offer virtual tours of rental properties on the Internet and one of the areas first to offer online reservations.

In 2006 the company employed approximately sixty-five full-time employees and independent real estate agents. It also provides seasonal employment for an additional 250 people. Kaiser Realty is the oldest family-owned vacation rental management and real estate sales company operating under the leadership of the original founder and owner in the Gulf Shores/ Orange Beach area. The company celebrated its

RIVIERA
UTILITIES

Riviera Utilities traces its roots to October 2, 1916, when the City of Foley entered into an agreement with Swanstrom Brothers Saw Mill to install twelve 50-watt streetlights for $60 and to furnish electrical current for $15 per month.

The Swanstrom Brothers, who had recently purchased a used 100-volt generator to supply electric lights for the mill, saw an opportunity to cash in—albeit in a small way—on their capital improvement.

The street lighting installation was completed in December and Foley paid its first electric bill on January 2, 1917, heralding the start of public utility service in that section of the city. The city then began considering purchasing a lighting plant of its own, and on December 21, 1917, voters unanimously (19-0) approved issuing $3,000 in general obligation bonds to purchase a light plant and wire downtown.

Orville Orr was low bidder ($161.40) on the light plant building and F. W. Walker was low bidder ($115.47) on the job of erecting the distribution system. The two 15-kilowatt Delco units rated at 100 volts DC (direct current) along with all other supplies and materials cost $2,266.11.

The plant—completed in June 1918—launched Foley into the electric business. The plant's generating capacity in those days

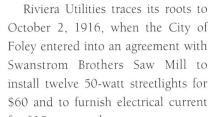

Above: Riviera Utilities office building at 700 Whispering Pines Road in Daphne, Alabama.

Below: Riviera Utilities lineman complete work on a pole that will provide distribttion service to the new office building in Foley.

could not electrify two modern homes. The city made electricity available in mid afternoon and turned it off in the evening at eleven. It charged customers $1.85 a month minimum and eighteen cents straight per kilowatt-hour.

In November 1919, the city called another election to authorize an additional $1,800 in general obligation bonds to purchase a 25-horsepower engine and alternating current generator rated at 15 kilowatts. The DC units installed were limited in their ability to transmit electricity over distance.

Once again voters approved the bond issue unanimously (14-0). The city's lighting system struggled financially. By 1922 the city realized it would either need to raise rates or sell the property. It incorporated its electric generating plant as the Foley Light & Power Company with capital consisting of $7,500. On July 24, 1922, voters approved selling the business by a vote of 61-1, and on August 23, 1922, J. B. Foley purchased the system for $6,000, an amount that represented the electric company's outstanding debt.

Items the city sold included a powerhouse consisting of an 18-foot-by-22-foot building located where the South Baldwin Chamber of Commerce building is located, two Delco generators, 54 battery cells, one 25-horsepower Fairbanks-Morse Model "Y" oil engine, one 15-kilowatt Fairbanks-Morse compound-wound generator, 150 poles, 15,000 feet of insulated wire, 50 DC meters and 30 insulators.

From that date until July 28, 1941, several private interests operated the electric company.

On February 10, 1929, Central States Edison Company, which owned Foley Light & Power Company at the time, formed Riviera Utilities Corporation. The Public Utilities Holding Company Act, passed by Congress in 1935, forced Central States Edison to sell the utility. Foley repurchased the business using revenue anticipation bonds, a funding instrument authorized by Alabama voters for just such an event. The city also bought Baldwin County Electric Light and Power Company, completing both transactions on July 28, 1941.

The Foley Municipal Electric Utilities Board, consisting of three members (five members sit on the board now), began operating the utilities on July 1, 1952. It also began operating the water system and portions of the sanitary sewer system owned by the City of Foley.

Today, Riviera Utilities has expanded its service to provide electricity, water, wastewater, natural gas and television cable services within the city's corporate limits. Along with its main office at 413 East Laurel Avenue in Foley, the utility operates a branch office at 700 Whispering Pines Road in Daphne. Electrical infrastructure includes 100 miles of transmission lines, 1,500 miles of overhead distribution lines, more than 200 miles of underground distribution lines and 22 substations at 19 locations.

Riviera Utilities provides electrical service to Spanish Fort, Daphne, Point Clear, and portions of Fairhope, Loxley, Summerdale, Foley, Elberta, Lillian, Magnolia Springs and Bon Secour. Run by a general manager, the utility also provides service to the City of Foley with water, gas, wastewater and cable television.

As for the future, Riviera Utilities plans to upgrade three substations and build four new ones to serve the growth that South Baldwin County is experiencing. The utility is in the process of upgrading or replacing miles of transmission and distribution lines. These improvements will bolster reliability and provide electrical capacity for many years to come.

Above: Riviera Utilities lineman complete the connections on transmission poles for the substation service in the city of Loxley, Alabama.

Below: Riviera Utilities main office located at 413 East Laurel Avenue in Foley, Alabama.

OAK HAVEN COTTAGES

If you ever have to spend some time in the Deep South, then Oak Haven cottages in Fairhope, Alabama is the ideal place to stay, whether it is just a short business stop-over, or a drawn-out vacation, or a seasonal escape from the cold Northern winter.

The sixteen Oak Haven cottages are ideally located on the slope from the center of Fairhope to the shores of Mobile Bay. The Bay connects the Mobile River—the largest river system east of the Mississippi—to the Gulf of Mexico, which generates a year-round pleasant subtropical climate and environment.

The cottages are between Fairhope's Municipal Park, the city pier, and the city beach, all just within a few minutes walking distance. Each of the sixteen single and duplex cottages has screened porches, decks, and fully equipped kitchens with dishes, cookware, microwave, coffeemaker and toaster. Linen and towels are available. Each living room has a hide-a-bed and cable television. All cottages have air conditioning. In short, they are a wonderful "home away from home."

Shopping is simple—the center of city of Fairhope is only ten minutes walking distance away—and its stores are geared to visitors.

Fishing, boating and water sports are a tradition in this area so rich in sea life. The Bay abounds in fish and other seafood, and deep-sea excursions are a daily routine. It is a fisherman's paradise. If you are lucky you may even experience a "Jubilee," a unique natural phenomenon where literally millions of bottom fish like flounders, crabs, eels, shrimps, and other Bay denizens beach themselves on the Eastern shore of the Bay, and are picked up in bucket-quantities by the happy shore-town people.

Fairhope's artist colony will please the taste of culturally interested visitors; there is always something going on: concerts, plays, lectures, and much more. The city has places of worship of all major denominations. The city's culinary offerings have built a reputation in the area.

Historically, the region is rich with nearly two centuries of legend and heritage. Originally the Oak Haven lots were part of a land grant. Its log cabins were acquired in 1982 by Port Captain R. Neise who made considerable improvements. His wife Meriam, a native of Hawaii, attends to the guests and guarantees their pleasant stay at the Oak Haven Cottages.

You just must come down to have a wonderful time—alone, or with your family or friends. As they say down here: "Y'all come!"

WEICHERT, REALTORS®– SEA-N-SHORE

WEICHERT, REALTORS®–Sea-N-Shore strives to be the leading real estate company in Baldwin County by providing customers and clients with the most rewarding real estate experience through comprehensive services that satisfy even their unexpressed needs and wants.

A full-service real estate company, originally WEICHERT, REALTORS®–Sea-N-Shore was known as Sea-N-Shore Management, Inc. Sea-N-Shore's primary services at that time were a vacation rental and property management company in addition to a linen and laundry service.

Pat Callihan of Marathon, Florida, Gary Owen of Ann Arbor, Michigan and Ron Owen of Orange Beach, Alabama founded the company in April 1985. Their original project was the development of the condominium project, The Whaler. The development of The Whaler was a landmark event for future developments along Alabama's Gulf Coast by establishing in the Alabama judicial system that condominium views adjacent to the developed property are not protected under Alabama Law. When the 1985 real estate market became economically depressed, several purchasers forfeited their earnest money and did not buy the units they had contracted for. Ron met the challenge by convincing the construction loan company to furnish the unsold units and put them in a vacation rental program and rent the units. Thus Sea-N-Shore Management was formed.

Many significant events occurred during the eighties in Gulf Shores and Orange Beach. Ron

*Above: A sales rally, Loxley,
Alabama 2006.*

Below: President Nick Wilmott.

recalls a meeting when a group of town leaders gathered and discussed whether or not to keep this area a secret or to go forward and become a resort area and attract tourists from all over the country. The decision was made to become a resort attraction and Ron decided at that point to grow Sea-N-Shore Management.

During this same time period, the Moonraker Motel (which is now a condominium) located on West Beach was purchased, in addition to a couple of very small rental companies in Gulf Shores. Sea-N-Shore was now a full fledge vacation rental and property management company renting condominiums and managing the Moonraker as a twenty-four-hour motel. For added income, Ron ran a linen service out of the small laundry room of the Moonraker, providing linen to some of the other management companies on the island. Throughout the eighties and early nineties, they have managed ten major condominium projects, as well as developed and sold seven more condominium projects in Orange Beach, including Flamingo Key, Marlin Key, Dolphin Key, Dolphin Harbor, Sandy Cove, The Enclave, and Sapphire Beach.

In the late 1980s Donna Owen, Ron's wife joined the ownership of Sea-N-Shore, replacing Pat and Gary. Then in 1997, Ron and Donna Owen's son, Nick Wilmott joined the family business as a sales agent after receiving his real estate license at the age of nineteen, helping sell the condominiums that Ron developed. In 2000, after graduating from the University of Alabama, Nick officially joined the family business full-time as Manager of Vacation Rentals and Sales. Ron moved forward with developments, while Nick and Donna increased the rentals and sales side of the business.

By 2002, Nick had followed in his father's footsteps by taking control and ownership of Sea-N-Shore. Nick cannot help but smile every day as he starts his days running the company his parents founded, sitting at the desk he once slept under, as a child, waiting on his mom to finish working.

In 2004, after Hurricane Ivan destroyed approximately seventy percent of the properties managed, the decision was made to affiliate with WEICHERT, REALTORS®, a national franchise whose main concentration is along the East Coast and South Florida and focus strictly on sales and development.

As a new franchise with Weichert Real Estate Affiliates in 2004, newly named WEICHERT, REALTORS®, Sea-N-Shore expanded their company's presence north of the beach and a year later, opened a second branch in Robertsdale, Alabama.

With a motto of "Weichert Works!" the firm offers a comprehensive array of services including real estate sales, property management and development consulting.

The company prides itself on its training and agent development courses that sales agents of all levels of experience can utilize. From Fast Track and Success Track, brand new agents right out of real estate school can learn the basic fundamentals of real estate sales, while

Mentoring Programs give those experienced agents a chance to learn and teach while doing their every day sales.

Always looking forward to the future, WEICHERT, REALTORS®–Sea-N-Shore has set goals for their offices that call for continued growth in all areas. Future plans include opening additional offices in Fort Morgan, Foley, and Orange Beach.

For additional information or to find out what is available in Baldwin County, visit Sea-N-Shore's Web site at www.SeaNShore.com or www.Weichert.com.

❖

Above: Habitat for Humanity REALTORS® Build, Foley, Alabama.

Below: Company mascot "Kurt" visiting McCarron Insurance.

View of Gulf not a right, judge rules

9/20/84

Alabama law "does not give anybody the right to a view" of the Gulf of Mexico according to Baldwin County Circuit Judge Floyd Enfinger.

The judge issued a directed verdict Thursday, on the request of Whaler Condominiums and the town of Gulf Shores, ordering the jury to find a Gulf Shores zoning ordinance granted March 12 by the Gulf Shores Board of Adjustment to Whaler developer Forrest Waters Jr. of Fort Deposit.

The variance allowed Waters to disregard a 20 foot setback requirement and build all the way to the property line on the beach.

"I found under Alabama law that Gulf House Association (represented by Taylor "Red" Wilkins Jr. of Bay Minette) presented no legal evidence why the variance for the south setback line should not be granted," Enfinger said.

Waters testified Wednesday that he and two partners have already spent $1.4 million in the $3.6 million seven story condominium project on East Beach. He said after the trial this week he hoped Enfinger's ruling would be the end of the year long battle between neighbors.

However, Wilkins said it's not over yet. He plans to appeal Thursday's ruling to the Alabama Court of Civil Appeals in Montgomery.

Gulf House sought a perma-

Whaler site

Last week, a Baldwin County Circuit Court judge ruled that Alabama law "does not give anybody the right to a view" of the Gulf of Mexico. The judge then issued a directed verdict ordering the jury to find a Gulf Shores zoning ordinance legal in favor of the Whaler Condominium in Gulf Shores, above left, but lawyers for the Gulf House Association plan to appeal the decision.

JOE RALEY BUILDERS, INC.

Beginning his career as a carpenter's helper in 1955, Joe Raley never dreamed that fifty years later his self-named custom home, condominium, and commercial building company would be one of the fastest growing businesses of its kind in Baldwin County. Back in 1975, Joe opened Joe Raley Builders with just three employees. Today, Joe's son Scott Raley is president of the company, and his grandson, Brad Raley, serves as vice president. Together, the three generations have grown the company to employee dozens of full-time workers and hundreds of sub-contractors. In addition, Joe Raley Builders has enjoyed a growth in revenues of $10 million in 2001 to $80 million in 2006.

According to Joe, development on the Island began to dramatically change after Hurricane Frederick in 1979. One year later, Joe Raley Builders constructed one of the first condominiums on the Island at a time when no one even knew what a condominium was. Joe remembers well that a two-bedroom/two bath beachfront unit at Island Shores sold for $49,000. The company soon constructed several more condominiums and hotels including the original Light House, Youngs By The Sea and Oleander. The company built the first bay front condominium in 1981, Back Bay Condominium. Commercial projects in the early eighties included the well known seafood

restaurant Sea & Suds, as well as the Alabama Gulf Coast Chamber of Commerce Welcome Center on Highway 59. Joe oversaw the construction of the Welcome Center and donated time, materials and labor to the project while encouraging other companies to assist the Chamber in their effort to bring more visitors to the beautiful Alabama coast.

In recent years, under the direction of Scott, the company has flourished building

Above: Joe, Scott, Brad, and Bryan Raley.

Below: Construction of Bama Bayou.

hundreds of custom homes, condominiums and commercial projects. Joe Raley Builders, Inc. was the first company to construct a condominium project on the Bon Secour River, and the company presented the first mixed-use project to be constructed on the Intracoastal Waterway, Bama Bayou. Bama Bayou is a proposed $300 million-plus project that includes over 1,100 condominium units, a 68,000 +/- (gross) square foot convention center, over 150,000 +/- square feet of retail, restaurants, a marina, amphitheater, nature center, and exciting entertainment including Gulf World, where visitors can swim with a dolphin, and Bayou Beach, a world-class water park. The company is also responsible for some of the largest, most luxurious condominium units on the Island, the 4,500 +/- square-foot, multimillion-dollar units at Oceania on West Beach Boulevard in Gulf Shores.

Joe Raley Builders is quickly becoming well known across the Southeast for its high quality work. Currently, the company has numerous projects planned for the Alabama Gulf Coast, as well as North Alabama and the Florida Panhandle. Joe Raley Builders is planning to develop and construct a condo/hotel in Panama City Beach, Florida. Plans call for a well known, national hotel chain to have its name on nearly 200 units connected to Gulf World Marine Park in Panama City Beach.

Joe Raley Builders' sister company R & R Contracting LLC, was formed in 2004 and today has over 140 employees with projects underway in Alabama, Mississippi, Georgia and Florida. P & R Excavating LLC, another sister company of Joe Raley Builders, employs over thirty people and has numerous projects across the Alabama Gulf Coast.

Through the years, Joe Raley Builders has found numerous ways to give back to the community from constructing the first ballparks in Orange Beach and Summerdale to its most current community project, Youth-Reach Gulf Coast. The company is involved in the development and construction of Youth-Reach Gulf Coast, a Christian ministry designed to change the lives of troubled teens.

For more information about Joe Raley Builders, Inc., visit www.joeraleybuilders.com.

Above: A Joe Raley Builders' custom home.

Below: A Joe Raley Builders' condominium.

BALDWIN COUNTY SCHOOL DISTRICT

History is alive and well in the Baldwin County School District and embodies a rich legacy of landmarks that are still being written today.

Baldwin County is the home of the first public school in Alabama, built at Boatyard Lake in 1799 by John Pierce to provide a place to educate the children of the community. This heritage of roots in small community schools has permeated the philosophy of the Baldwin County Public School system throughout its existence. The school system logo highlights the pride in the foundation of public schools since 1799 and the focus on the continued priority place on "Building Excellence."

Today the school system is operated under the leadership of a seven member elected School Board and an appointed Superintendent, Dr. Faron L. Hollinger, the eleventh in a line of superintendents who have led to a ranking among the top educational systems in the south. Now one of the fastest growing in Alabama, with more than 26,800 students (3,900 with special needs) and 3,800 employees on 46 campuses, it is the recipient of numerous recognitions and awards for accomplishments and excellence. The system's school campuses are located in seven distinct communities, each feeding into one of the seven high schools in the county: Gulf Shores, Foley, Robertsdale, Fairhope, Daphne, Spanish Fort, and Baldwin County High in Bay Minette.

Most impressive is the Little Red Schoolhouse Project, the restoration of the Blakeley School, now located at the system office complex. The building is a tribute to the emphasis placed on education by families throughout the county. The school was built by African-American families in the Bromley Community and was saved under the leadership of former Superintendent Dr. Leslie Smith, who led the initial movement to preserve the building.

The Living History museum is open for student field trips; students experience life in school grades

first through eighth in a 1921 setting. Volunteers of the Retired Educators Association make history come alive for the students. The program is under the direction of Harriet Outlaw, Special Projects Administrator for the school system.

The history project has also worked with the County Commission Department of Archives and History to record school history through a series of DVD presentations airing on cable television. The project has garnered nationwide attention due oral histories to preserve the memories of former students and teachers of buildings, which are more than fifty years old. The preservation of the memories associated with the older buildings is enhanced by the production of this video series.

The first "large" schools built in the county were in the towns of Bay Minette, Foley, Robertsdale, and Fairhope, appearing on the scene by 1915. These were designated as high schools as they served students grades first through twelfth. Eventually,

more than ninety rural schools were consolidated as larger schools were built in the 1930s.

African-American education was originally operated under the direction of the Baldwin County Board of Education. There were at least fourteen black community schools in the county serving grades first through eighth. After completion of this phase of their education, students could attend Baldwin County Training School in Daphne, Alabama and live in the boarding facilities provided there.

The school in Daphne was originally founded by the Eastern Shore Baptist Missionary Association and the oldest building onsite is now dedicated to become an African American Education Museum for Baldwin County. In 1950, two additional African American High Schools were built; Aaronville in Foley, and Douglasville in Bay Minette. These three African American high schools were consolidated with other area schools in 1968-69.

At least two "Teacherages" are in existence today. This housing was often provided by the county to entice principal/teachers to the rural areas. Stapleton and Elsanor Schools both use former teacherages as schoolrooms today.

Recently, the office buildings in Bay Minette were named in honor of former Superintendents Dr. R. L. McVay, Dr. Candler McGowan, and S. M. Tharp. The portrait gallery of superintendents is housed in the Office of the Superintendent and includes the first female Superintendent in Alabama, Lillie Wetzell, who served the system in 1918.

Today, the Baldwin County School District is providing new schools at a rate never before seen in the county. In the past five years alone teachers have increased to 1,913; a $270 million capitol improvement is underway; $23 million in school renovations have been completed; the District has received one of the highest *Standard and Poors* financial ratings for school systems in Alabama and is one of only fifteen school systems nationally honored by the *American School Board Journal* for use of technology in the classroom.

Nothing less than "World Class Education" is the twenty-first century goal for Baldwin County Public School.

For more information about the school system, visit the Baldwin County School District on the Internet at www.bcbe.org.

CRAFT FARMS

Seeds...small pieces of something that, when planted in the right environment; flourishes and beautifies everything around it. One could say Craft Farms began as a seed in the Gulf Shores area and anyone who's ever visited will tell you it definitely has flourished and done more to beautify the area than just about anything else that has been established in the region.

After moving to the Gulf Shores area in 1953, founder, R.C. Craft purchased 870 acres of farmland just three miles from the sugar beaches of sleepy Gulf Shores, Alabama. In the mid-1960s, R.C. began growing gladiolas on the property and gradually incorporated new crops such as corn, soybeans, and snap beans while always hoping the land would eventually have value beyond farming.

In 1974, his son Robert, an agricultural business student at Auburn University, wanted to enhance the family farming operation with a stable year-round crop. That opportunity came with the passing of Cole Brown, a local farmer who had 100 acres of land profitably growing

Above: Cypress Bend Par 3, hole 6.

Below: Cotton Creek, hole 6.

centipede grass. Robert had worked during his college years for the family of a fraternity brother in the turf business, so partnering with his father; he leased Cole's land and Craft Turf Farms was formed. By 1980, all 870 acres of the land owned by the Crafts had evolved into a turf farm.

Although the primary turf market for Craft Farms was, and still is, residential wholesale, they also supplied Bermuda grass to athletic fields and golf courses. The entire Craft Family had always enjoyed golf and it was at this point that they began to consider the possibility of building a golf course in Gulf Shores. Due to the strong business relationships held between R.C. and the community, coupled with their ownership of the land just three miles from the quickly developing beaches, the transition from turf to golf seemed an easy stretch.

Although they had the excitement and a playing knowledge of the sport of golf, R.C. and Robert realized it was going to take someone experienced in both development and golf course design to convince any potential financial backers—that's when the legendary Arnold Palmer stepped into the picture making Craft Farms home to the only Palmer Signature golf courses in Alabama.

Cotton Creek opened in 1988 as part of the 650-acre lot, master-planned Craft Farms community. Palmer managed the course the first three years. After the initial three years,

the Craft family began running the facility instilling their personal touches, which are still unmistakably evident today. Cotton Creek was the area's first resort golf course and has continued as an area leader adding nine more Palmer holes in 1992 and another nine in 1998, which together became Cypress Bend, hailed by *Golf Digest* as the "Number 1 Most Playable New Course in the U.S." Accentuated by the premier Cypress Point condominiums, a Courtyard by Marriott and also home to the McCollough Institute for Health and Appearance, Craft Farms has become one of the finest golf destinations on the Alabama Gulf Coast.

The latest additions to the property include the transformation of sixty acres of commercial property along Highway 59 into a home for a fourteen theater Cobb Cinema, a new Target store and The Pinnacle at Craft Farms Shopping Center. While all residential property within Craft Farms proper has been sold, 400 acres north of Craft Farms is being developed into another outstanding residential community. Craft Farms North, as it is called, has experienced great success and Phase I sold out within months. Adjacent to the Foley Beach Express, Craft Farms North is sure to be a success.

Since its beginning, Craft Farms has been an inviting place where the friendly hospitality is as warm as the golf is challenging. The Craft's traditional values continue to play a major role throughout its operations and Craft Farms is one of South Baldwin's greatest success stories. Be sure to experience "Golf As It Was Meant To Be Played" whenever you visit the Alabama Gulf Coast.

For more information please visit Craft Farms on the web at www.craftfarms.com.

Above: A beautiful day compliments of Cypress Bend, hole 18.

Below: The clubhouse at Cotton Creek.

FAULKNER STATE COMMUNITY COLLEGE

For over forty years, generations of students and faculty have found their place in the education legacy of Alabama's Faulkner State Community College, a public two-year institution located on campuses situated in Bay Minette, the administrative campus, Gulf Shores, and Fairhope. The

College, one of thirteen original two-year colleges created by an act of the Alabama Legislature in 1963, is under the authority of the State Board of Education. Faulkner State is a member of the Alabama College System, a group of twenty-six public two-year colleges and one upper division college.

Faulkner State has undergone several transitions and name changes in its lifetime. During the first months in operation, the college was called Bay Minette State Junior College, but early in 1966 the State Board of Education renamed the College William Lowndes Yancey State Junior College to honor a pre-Civil War statesman and educator.

In 1970 the school was christened James H. Faulkner State Junior College to honor one of Baldwin County's most prominent citizens. The college finally became Faulkner State Community College in August 1992 to more accurately reflect its modern mission and purpose.

Faulkner State has grown from an initial enrollment of 401 students and one campus in 1965 to a 2007 combined enrollment of 4,000 students among all three campuses. The college began offering courses at Fairhope in 1970 and, in 1975, added a permanent staff and student services, as well as the expansion of programs and services to the community.

The Fairhope Campus has been housed both at the Fairhope High School and at the old Fairhope Library Building. In 1987 the present Fairhope site was acquired, which originally served as the home of the Marietta Johnson School of Organic Education. The site was entered in the National Register of Historic Places in the United States Department of Interior on July 1, 1988.

In 1985 the college opened a site in Foley and moved to the present Gulf Shores Campus location in the Fall of 1993.

Faulkner State Community College has an open-door admission policy and is committed to the professional and cultural growth of each student without regard to race, color, gender, disability, religion, creed, national origin or age. The college serves to provide an educational environment that promotes development and learning through a wide variety of educational programs and instructional strategies, adequate and comfortable facilities, a caring and well-qualified staff, flexible scheduling, and convenient locations.

Faulkner State Community College provides ten different divisions of study: Fine Arts (Art, Graphic Arts, Music, and Speech), Office and Legal Administrative (Office Administration or Paralegal), Social Sciences (Criminal Justice, Economics, History, Political Science, Psychology, and Sociology), Natural Science (Astronomy, Biology, Chemistry, Physical Science, and Physics),

Health, Physical Education and Recreation (Health and Physical Education), Nursing and Allied Health (Dental Assisting, Nursing, Surgical Tech and Paramedic), Business and Computer Science (Accounting, Computer Science, and Management Supervision Technology), Mathematics and Pre-Engineering (Mathematics and Pre-Engineering), Language Arts Division (Developmental English, English and Reading), and Hospitality Administration (Culinary Arts, Hotel and Restaurant Management, Pastry/Baking/Confectionary, Golf Course Management, and Landscape Technology). Students may earn an Associate in Arts Degree, an Associate in Science Degree, and an Associate in Applied Science Degree or a Certificate in a chosen occupational/vocational/technical program. Faulkner State Community College also offers a number of courses over the Internet.

Over the years, the College has continued to expand its vision for students and the surrounding communities. In 2006 the state-of-the-art Sun Chief Hall, a $13.6 million student residence hall, was opened to accommodate 320 students. Each room includes a privacy wall and full bath, as well as wireless Internet. The Sun Chief Hall's main floor includes four fireplaces and comfortable sitting areas, a computer lab/study room, a theater, and a fully equipped game room.

The college completed the Lady Sun Chief Softball Stadium on the Bay Minette campus in 2006. It includes handicapped accessible areas and a 260-seat capacity with stadium chairs.

In 2007 the Fairhope campus expanded its successful RN nursing program with new classes beginning spring 2008.

For more information about Faulkner State Community College please visit www.faulknerstate.edu on the Internet or call 1-800-231-3752.

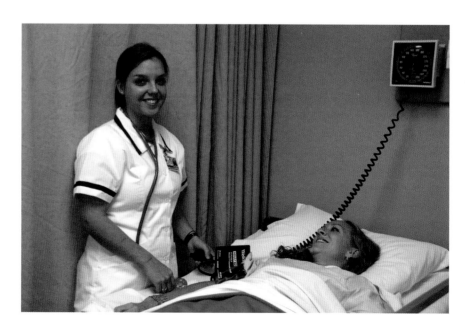

DAUPHIN REALTY

Dauphin Realty began with a vision to create a real estate company in the Mobile/Baldwin area that would not only be the best, but also hold the highest caliber of management, employees and agents. In 1986 the company was founded with Mickie Russell acting as manager broker for the new company. Six months later, Gayle Grabert was hired as an administrative assistant and is now the sales manager of the corporate office.

Today, Mickie serves as president and owner of Dauphin Realty of Mobile, Inc., Dauphin Realty of Baldwin Company, Inc. and Dauphin Realty Bayside, Inc. Her acquisition of the Baldwin County office came with many transitions that first began in 1963 with the partnership of J.V. Cummings and Walter M. Wilson. Five years later, a new office was built at 559 North Section Street. Cummings decided to sell out to Wilson, who brought Dorothy "Dot" Y. Yeager in as his partner. Wilson & Yeager bought a Century 21 franchise; Lee Masterson joined in the partnership; and Century 21–Wilson, Yeager & Masterson was born. A decade later, the company was sold and eventually Wilson retired and sold his share to Yeager & Masterson.

With its continued growth and expansion, Dauphin Realty realized the need for a presence on the Eastern Shore, so the company approached Dot about purchasing Yeager & Masterson in Fairhope. The purchase came to fruition in 1992. At the age of 82, Dot continues to play a vital role in the agency and consistently maintains her status as one of the company's Top Agents. She has been named Realtor of the Year and is a past president of the Baldwin County Association of Realtors.

The office at 559 North Section Street has been enlarged four times since its construction and the Eastern Shore office has continued to prosper, commanding a large percentage of

❖

Above: Dorothy Y. Yeager.

Below: Mickie Russell.

the market in the Eastern Shore area and Baldwin County.

Today, Dauphin Realty has offices in Mobile at 2569 Dauphin Street, in West Mobile at 6207 Cottage Hill Road and in Fairhope at 559 North Section Street (Baldwin County) and 19452 Scenic Highway 98 (Bayside). Over the years, it has grown from one agent in a one room office to eighty agents, eleven office staff, four offices and a five-member management team with more than 100 years combined experience in the real estate business.

Dauphin Realty is involved in each of its branch communities and is a member of such organizations as the Eastern Shore Chamber of Commerce, the Board of Advisors for the Mobile Chamber of Commerce, St. Jude's Children's Hospital and St. Mary's School, to name a few.

The future of Dauphin Realty is as bright as ever—the company is proud to maintain its status as number three in the Mobile/Eastern Shore market place and continues to embrace cutting edge technology in the field. And, as always, Dauphin Realty strives to create an environment of mutual trust and respect, honesty, enthusiasm and continued search for excellence. One of the company's main goals is to be large enough to provide the best resources in the real estate industry, but intimate enough to guarantee the highest level of quality service and professionalism. The provisions of integrity and dedication of service remain the foundation and cornerstone of Dauphin Realty.

For more information about Dauphin Realty, please visit them on the Internet at www.dauphinrealty.com.

❖

Dauphin Realty's Fairhope office.

COLONIAL BANK

Above: Colonial Bank's Baldwin County roots run deep. This location in Foley is built on the same site as the Farmers & Merchant Bank pictured below. Throughout the past two decades, Colonial has focused on building the communities we serve.

Below: The Farmers & Merchant Bank (as it looked in 1981) was first established in Baldwin County in the early 1930s.

At Colonial Bank, our goal is to provide the kind of banking experience that's hard to find these days. So we stay true to the one thing that we've always believed–banking is about people, not numbers.

As simple as that may sound, it has always been the key to our success in Baldwin County–and in each of our more than 320 banking offices in Alabama, Florida, Georgia, Nevada and Texas.

Colonial Bank began its relationship with the citizens of Baldwin County in 1986 when an agreement was reached between the Colonial BancGroup, Inc., and the stockholders of the local Farmers and Merchants Bank.

"This is a big step for us," Colonial Chairman and CEO Robert E. Lowder said at the time. "Farmers and Merchants is an established and growing bank, and it will have a very positive impact on our organization."

Farmers and Merchants Bank had served the Baldwin County area since 1932 and had offices in Foley, Gulf Shores, and Fairhope. Colonial has spent the subsequent two decades building on the success of that community bank by focusing on the people who live and work in the community.

Since 1986, Colonial Bank has added branches in Daphne, Lillian, Orange Beach, and second locations in Fairhope and Foley. The bank offers a broad line of retail and commercial

banking products and services including checking and savings accounts, personal and commercial loans, online banking, credit card, merchant services, and treasury management, as well as wealth management including asset management and estate planning solutions, money management products and insurance through Colonial Brokerage, Inc., and private banking services.

During its twenty year history in Baldwin County, Colonial has made other contributions to the communities of Baldwin County. In 1989 the Fairhope office transformed a potentially hazardous alley adjacent to its facility into a New Orleans-inspired patio courtyard that could be enjoyed by the whole community. Employees are also encouraged to take civic leadership roles, and Colonial has been involved in several charitable and civic projects from Relay for Life, to the United Way, to athletic sponsorships and local festivals. Our employees are people you know, who help make Baldwin

County a better place to live and a better place to bank.

The company has received numerous accolades. In 2007, Colonial was included in Forbes Magazine's Best Big Companies in America and in the publication's prestigious Global 1000 list. Colonial Bank is a subsidiary of the Colonial BancGroup, Inc., a $24-billion bank holding company based in Montgomery, Alabama. The company's common stock is traded on the New York Stock Exchange under the symbol CNB, and the company is located online at www.colonialbank.com.

Above: Colonial Bank currently has eight full-service locations in Baldwin County, including this office in Orange Beach.

Below: Colonial's Fairhope location contributes to the beauty of its surroundings. In 1989 the office transformed a potentially hazardous alley into a New Orleans-inspired patio and courtyard.

GULF SHORES
UTILITIES

The Utilities Board of the City of Gulf Shores, an agency of municipal government incorporated under Alabama state laws, is composed of seven Directors, appointed by the Mayor and confirmed by the City Council to serve staggered, six-year terms, without compensation.

This Board, which has full responsibility and authority for directing the utilities systems, closely coordinates its activities with the city.

In 1967 the three-member Water Works Board of the Town of Gulf Shores was issued $390,000 in revenue bonds to acquire the existing Gulf Shores water system, owned by the Town of Summerdale, and to construct additional facilities.

The acquisition included one 200 gallon-per-minute well and water treatment facility, a 50,000-gallon elevated tank, and a limited distribution system with a short section of six-inch main and other lines of four inches or smaller. Shortly afterward, the Board added a second well and 500 GPM water treatment facility.

Gulf Shores had no municipal sewer system until 1968, when the town built a 300 GPD, three-cell, lagoon system and laid lines to serve developed areas. The Water Works Board provided administration and operation.

Growth, including the development of Gulf State Park, necessitated utility system improvements and expansion in the 1970s. The Town of Gulf Shores formed a Water Supply Board and obtained a $700,000 Farmer's Home Administration loan in 1976 for the initial phases of the water well field north of the Intracoastal Waterway and the first phase of the Water Treatment Plant in north Gulf Shores.

By the end of the 1970s the water system had four wells and three water treatment facilities with a combined capacity of 2.5 MGD. The Gulf State Park water system

❖

Above: Water tank at Sportsplex.

Below: Administrative Office Building located at 149 East Sixteenth Avenue.

included a 500,000-gallon elevated tank. In addition to a 16-inch water line under the Intracoastal Waterway, a network of 6-, 8-, and 12-inch water lines served the area.

With hectic growth following Hurricane Frederick, the Town of Gulf Shores expanded the sewer system in the West Beach area and enhanced service capabilities elsewhere, while also facing stringent environmental requirements on the quality of water discharged from its treatment facility.

Gulf Shores formed the Governmental Utility Services Corporation (GUSC), vesting it with full ownership and responsibility for developing, administering and operating the wastewater system. GUSC issued $3.8 million in revenue bonds for major sewage collection, pumping, and transport facilities and a state-of-the-art wastewater treatment plant, the Gulf Shores Water Reclamation Facility (WRF). The plant, which began operating in 1987, can satisfactorily process 4 MGD of wastewater. It has established an exemplary performance record. Sewer service was extended into the Cypress Park area and north of the Intracoastal Waterway.

The Water Works Board responded aggressively to growth in the 1980s with new wells, treatment capability, transmission lines and water storage facilities. It issued over $5 million in revenue bonds to add water wells, expand water treatment capacity, build elevated and ground-level storage tanks and associated facilities, add major water and transmission lines, and extend the areas of water service.

GUSC and the Water Works Board consolidated in 1989 and became Gulf Shores Utilities. GSU became responsible for all area water and sewer demands. GSU has continued its predecessors' tradition of aggressive response to service demands and the addition of water and sewer system enhancements.

As of 2006, Gulf States Utilities had nine wells with a pumping capacity of 8.28 MGD, three treatment facilities with a capacity of 7.56 MGD, and eight water tanks with a combined capacity of 7.55 million gallons. The water system's average pumping rate in 2005 was 2.7 MGD, and GSU treated 1.02 billion gallons of water in 2004.

The wastewater plant has received state recognition for its operations. The Alabama Department of Environmental Management has issued it a discharge permit for 4 MGD. Upgrades consisting of two 3 MGD aeration basins with ultraviolet disinfection capability are planned in the near future to expand the plant to 6 MGD capability.

GSU continues to stay ahead of the growth in South Baldwin County, consistently upgrading, improving and extending water and wastewater systems.

The accomplishments of Gulf Shores Utilities have been attained by implementing cost-conscious, environmentally sensitive solutions to our needs so as to give credence to the phrase, "Gulf Shores, Bigger and Better."

ALABAMA GULF COAST AREA CHAMBER OF COMMERCE

The Gulf Shores Tourist Association was formed on the island in April 1966. For many years this organization operated with the focus of promoting tourism to the area. The association operated as a membership organization but also received funds from the City of Gulf Shores and the State of Alabama. The building, which housed the Tourist Association, was one of the first Welcome Centers in Alabama.

After Hurricane Frederic in 1979, the Tourist Association saw the need to focus on other aspects that were not directly related to tourism and in June 1981 the name Alabama Gulf Coast Area Chamber of Commerce was registered. In November of the same year, the chamber began to officially conduct business.

The Alabama Gulf Coast Area Chamber of Commerce was created to promote the entire island area. At the time, Gulf Shores was the only incorporated area of the island. Membership dues and a commitment from the City of Gulf Shores provided funding for the new chamber. Once Orange Beach incorporated, they began contributing funds to the operating account of the Chamber.

In late 1986 the Alabama Gulf Coast Area Chamber of Commerce supported the annexation of the Gulf State Park into the corporate limits of Gulf Shores. Many business people in the newly incorporated Orange Beach disagreed with the action. In December 1986 the Orange Beach Chamber of Commerce was formed with a focus on supporting the businesses of Orange Beach. The contract for funding to support the Alabama Gulf Coast Area

Chamber of Commerce was rescinded. At a later date, the City of Orange Beach began funding the new Orange Beach Chamber of Commerce.

The City of Gulf Shores continued to support the efforts of the Alabama Gulf Coast Area Chamber of Commerce through monetary investment and supported the chamber with partial funding for the Welcome Center expansion in 1990.

Because of the need for dedicated marketing dollars, in 1992 the Alabama Gulf Coast Area Chamber of Commerce began to explore the feasibility of forming a Convention & Visitors Bureau separate from the chamber. The Convention & Visitors Bureau would be funded by a percentage of lodging tax dollars and the chamber would be supported by membership dues. After months of discussion and negotiations the Alabama Gulf Coast Convention & Visitors Bureau became a reality in November 1993.

During discussions on the formation of the Convention & Visitors Bureau, negotiations began to formally merge the Orange Beach Chamber of Commerce and the Alabama Gulf Coast Area Chamber of Commerce. This was accomplished and on December 31, 1993, the two chambers were officially merged. Today the chamber is funded totally by membership dues and revenue generated from special events such as the Annual National Shrimp Festival. The Alabama Gulf Coast Area Chamber of Commerce is the only chamber in the county that does not receive funding from any municipality.

After the merger was complete, the combined Alabama Gulf Coast Area Chamber of Commerce had 350 members. Membership has continued to increase and as of December 31, 2007, the chamber had slightly over 1000 members.

"Foley, the Forward City!" Among Alabama's many beautiful and inviting Gulf Coast communities, the city of Foley has been defined by what those words mean for well over a hundred years. When the slogan was officially adopted in 1977, it combined what historian Doris Rich described as "the most successful pioneers" of the late nineteenth century with a hope and vitality that has sustained this flourishing community and its many citizens into the twenty-first century.

It is true that a history of any community is not really about places and events, but it is about its people—those original settlers who sought a new life among the lush pine forests and abundant waterways. It is about proud, hardworking families and leaders who continue to honor Foley by preserving its rich heritage and ensuring its vital place throughout the region.

Named in honor of John Burton Foley, who first visited the area early in 1902 and used much of his own money to create many of the area's first roads, schoolhouses, working mills, and farms. The city was officially founded in 1905 and incorporated in 1915. This was a "planned city" from the very beginning and with its year-round mild climate and fertile setting; Foley soon blossomed. By 1909, Rich writes that *The Onlooker* described the town as already having "a new 20 room hotel...two general stores...two sawmills,

good school, local and long distance telephones...weekly newspaper, bakery, jeweler...and two churches." From the start, it was clear that Foley would never stand still.

Today, the city has become a crossroads to all areas of the coastal region and is a central destination for those living in the surrounding communities as well as tourists from around the world. The economic center of the South Baldwin area, Foley is something of a "mini-metropolis" with its large library, the South Baldwin Regional Medical Center, civic center, high school and numerous museums, galleries and antique shops nestled among a growing population of 10,000. The city boasts an active spirit of volunteerism with South Baldwin County United Way supporting thirty area programs, a Salvation Army, South Baldwin Scouting Association and numerous civic organizations.

In his descriptive and engaging historical work, *Foley Steps Forward*, Tom Stoddard writes, "But Foley has something—an attitude, a way of approaching things—that has indeed moved it 'forward'...it has become the main seat of commerce, a manufacturing and transportation hub, and a destination of tourists and shoppers from throughout the nation."

It is little wonder that a city firmly rooted in its exciting history and proudly looking ahead to its limitless future is described as, "Foley, the Forward City!"

CITRIN LAW FIRM P.C.

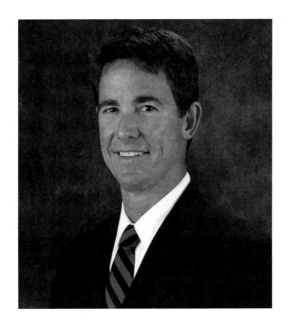

❖

Top, left: Andrew T. Citrin

Top, right: Elizabeth A. Citrin.

Below: Steven P. Savarese.

Bottom: The offices of the Citrin Law Firm, P.C.

Andrew T. Citrin, born in Hollywood, Florida, graduated from Tulane University in New Orleans with a B.A. in economics in 1983. While at Tulane, Citrin served as president of the Kappa Sigma Fraternity. He then attended Cumberland School of Law in Birmingham, Alabama, where he served as articles editor for the *American Journal of Trial Advocacy* and served on the Moot Court and the Trial Advocacy Boards. He graduated cum laude, and in 1986 he was inducted into the Curia Honoris Society by the law school faculty.

Citrin began his career as an appellate lawyer for the prestigious trial firm Cunningham, Bounds, Yance, Crowder & Brown, where he handled numerous landmark cases before the Alabama and U.S. Supreme Courts. After ten years of high profile appellate work, Citrin shifted his practice to trial work, specializing in serious injury and death cases.

In 1998, Citrin moved to historic downtown Daphne where his law practice has blossomed into a full service trial firm. Citrin practices in all areas of damages litigation, with emphasis on personal injury, wrongful death and fraud cases arising out of truck and automobile wrecks, product liability, maritime accidents, and medical malpractice. He is on the registered Bar Registry of Preeminent Lawyers, is AV (top) Rated, was elected to the Multi-Million Dollar Advocates and is board certified as a civil trial lawyer by the National Board of Trial Advocacy.

Elizabeth A. Citrin was born in Hollywood, Florida, and graduated with a B.A. in fine arts and economics from Vanderbilt University in 1981. After several years as a television producer and writer for CBS News, Lifetime Television, and WWOR TV, among others, Elizabeth entered law school, graduated from Pace University School of Law in White Plains, New York, in 1994. While at Pace, she studied environmental law under Robert F. Kennedy, Jr., and served as case note and comment editor of *Pace Law Review*. Elizabeth then served as a motions law clerk for the U.S. Court of Appeals for the Second Circuit, and then spent five years working as an assistant corporation counsel for the New York City Law Department, handling high-profile, high liability cases in the Special Litigation Unit. After the events of 9/11, Elizabeth moved with her two daughters to Daphne and worked for a large defense firm in Mobile until joining Citrin Law Firm, P.C. in 2004.

Steven P. Savarese joined the firm in 2006. He graduated from the University of Alabama with special honors in 2003, and from the University of Alabama School of Law in 2006. While in law school, he was awarded the George Peach Taylor Award for excellence in trial advocacy. He specializes in car and trucking accidents.

The Fairhope Chamber of Commerce was organized on June 6, 1924, with about thirty people in attendance. William McIntosh was elected president. Other officers were: Dr. V. M. Schowalter, first vice president; J. E. Gaston, second vice president; and R. F. Powell, third vice president. Trustees named were E. B. Gaston, C. C. Baldwin and H. P. Kemper, with George Martin named treasurer and O. K. Cummings, secretary.

The Chamber, even then, was actively involved in addressing the concerns of city sewer systems, beautification and most importantly at the time, the addition of a bridge connecting Mobile and Baldwin Counties. Today we are still tackling transit and technology concerns, among others through Blueprint for Tomorrow.

Aggressively involved in city and county matters, the Chamber remained active in the community, strengthening from the early thirty to forty members to over 100 members in 1943. In 1952 the board voted to change their name of the organization to the Fairhope and Eastern Shore Chamber of Commerce. It was incorporated in 1959 and the name changed again in February 1977 to the Eastern Shore Chamber of Commerce. Today

the Chamber serves communities from Historic Blakeley State Park, south to Weeks Bay—three municipalities and many unincorporated communities.

One of the Eastern Shore Chamber of Commerce's largest events, the Arts & Crafts Festival, began in 1953. In recent years the festival drew in excess of 250,000 people to the area and is named in the top ten festivals nationwide by *Sunshine Artist Magazine*. The event has an estimated $8 million impact to the region.

In 2006 the Chamber underwent a restructuring process as the result of a highly successful capital campaign. More than 100 volunteers raised $2 million dollars, above and beyond the original chamber budget, for a five-year strategic plan. Blueprint for Tomorrow addresses over fifty initiatives in six broad areas of concern—economic development, tourism, governmental affairs, education, transportation, and the environment, in partnership with the cities of Spanish Fort, Daphne, and Fairhope, and the Baldwin County Commission.

To find out more information about the Chamber, call (251) 621-8222 or 928-6387. Visit the website at www.eschamber.com.

David Clark, chairman of the Eastern Shore Chamber for 2007/08; Darrelyn Bender, president and CEO of the Chamber; and Joe Bullock, incoming chairman for 2008/09, standing in front of the Carl L. Bloxham building, named after the Chamber President serving from 1938-1940. The building, which is located on Fairhope Avenue in downtown Fairhope, Alabama, was donated to the Chamber in 1988. The Chamber also has an office located at the Scenic Overlook in Daphne, Alabama.

C&A Medical Inc.

Diabetic 1-Stop

C&A Medical Inc. and Diabetic 1-Stop are businesses truly born out of the care and love that founder, Carol Dolan-Groebe, feels for the population of senior adults in her area. Before she formed the business in 1992, Carol was employed with a company out of St. Louis, Missouri that provided Medicare covered supplies to nursing home patients.

When this company started a diabetic program, Carol decided to run an advertisement in the local senior newsletter—the response was overwhelming. Nearly overnight, she was seeing as many as thirty home patients in addition to her visits to the nursing homes. What surprised her was the connection she felt with each of her clients and how fond she grew of them. In fact, she cared so much that when the St. Louis company announced only four months into the program that it was being cancelled, Carol decided to apply to Medicare for her own provider number. Fifteen years later, C&A Medical processes insurance billing for diabetic testing supplies and Diabetic 1-Stop is a retail store carrying items that a person with diabetes might want or need.

Although Carol is the owner and president of the company, she is quick to note that without the help of many wonderful people, her business simply would not run. Her husband, Dennis, handles the considerable amount of billing and cousin Clara Baily Dolan, worked for

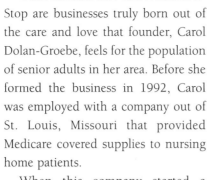

many years until her health forced her to retire. Office manager Carol Hollis "is the person who can, and will, do whatever is necessary." Shipping clerk, Marilyn Smith, "is a great gal who gets the job done." Elaine Bullock has just taken the important front office post as Mandy Watson decided to return to school. Sharon Byrne is their "Yankee girl" and handles all of the secondary insurance billing. Surely the most unusual on the list of important figures would have to be the company CEO Sophie, Carol's half-Shih Tzu and half-Chinese Pug, who comes to work every day and lets them know when it's time to eat, quit working and go home!

Carol's company is a labor of love. Diabetic 1-Stop moved into a storefront location to enable customers to see what is available to them and was created to help those customers living in rural areas and are unable to gain quick access to a walk-in store.

Looking back over the success of the businesses, Carol says, "All in all, the past fifteen years have been a pleasure for all of us here at C&A Medical and Diabetic 1-Stop."

In loving memory of Edmund D. Dolan, Sr. (1920-2006). We miss you.

The Flora-Bama Lounge & Package Inc. was the realization of a dream of the Tampary family who, in 1962, envisioned a lounge and package store for the new Florida/Alabama state line. Two years later, after construction of the Perdido Pass Bridge by the state of Alabama, which secured the western two miles of the Key from Florida, the original Flora-Bama was built.

In 1963 the state of Alabama completed the Perdido Pass Bridge and secured the western two miles of the Key from Florida. Set to open in the Spring of 1964, a fire consumed the Flora-Bama the day before its opening. Constantine Tampary with sons, Tony and Connie, rebuilt and officially opened the Flora-Bama in October of that same year. The Tamparys operated the business for fourteen successful years before selling to one of the current owners, Joe Gilchrist, in April 1978. In October 1984, Pat McClellan joined as a co-partner and vice president.

In September 2004, Hurricane Ivan damaged the main building of the Flora-Bama. Due to popular demand, the Flora-Bama reopened with the deck, top deck and courtyard areas in April 2005, while the rebuilding plans were finalized.

The Flora-Bama features "Good Times & Good Music" on three plus stages amidst a multileveled array of bars, shops, lottery sales and a five-star oyster bar and grill overlooking the beautiful Gulf of Mexico, located on the Florida/ Alabama line at 17401 Perdido Key Drive. Annual events at Flora-Bama include the Interstate Mullet Toss and Gulf Coast's Greatest Beach Party held the last full weekend in April and the Frank Brown International Songwriters' Festival held in November.

The Flora-Bama has earned its reputation as an international watering hole for folks of all walks of life with its simple motto: "To grant equal respect to all who enter." It is truly a celebration of diversity where friendships are renewed on each visit! For more information, visit their website at www.florabama.com.

Above: Post Ivan. c. September 2004.

Below: The last of the great American roadhouses.
COURTESY OF USA TODAY.

VOLKERT & ASSOCIATES, INC.

Organized in 1925 as Doullut & Ewin in New Orleans, the firm was purchased by Southern Industries after World War II and moved to Mobile, now the corporate headquarters. David G. Volkert, then president of Southern Industries, acquired the engineering company in 1954 and changed the name to David Volkert & Associates in 1963.

Volkert served actively in the company until his death in 2001. T. Keith King, P.E., became Volkert's president and CEO in 1983 and is now Chairman of the Board and CEO. Perry Hand serves as president and Chief Marketing Officer of the employee-owned company with over 700 employees.

Volkert provides engineering, surveys, environmental, landscape architecture, land planning, program management, and construction services from seventeen offices in nine states and the District of Columbia. Right of way and construction field offices are located throughout the firm's geographic service area.

Volkert formed the Baldwin County office with the acquisition of Perry Hand & Associates, a Gulf Shores engineering/survey firm established in 1972. The office moved to Foley in 2000 and now has a staff of fifty-five people including engineers, surveyors, land planners, landscape architects, environmental scientists, construction inspectors, design technicians, and support staff.

Clients include various municipalities in Baldwin County, the Baldwin County Commission, and private developers. A sample of projects designed by the Foley office includes: The Foley Beach Express, Roadway approaches to the bridge over the Canal; Craft Farms Golf Course Community in Gulf Shores; Peninsula Golf Course Community in Gulf Shores; Rock Creek Golf Course Community in Fairhope; Glenlakes Golf Course Community in Foley; Gulf State Park Campgrounds; The Beach Club; Renovations to Mobile Street and hiking trails along Mobile Bay in Fairhope; Foley Hike/Bike Trail; County Road 13, County Road 27 Extension in Spanish Fort, D'Olive Street Extension in Bay Minette; Renovations to Gulf Shores Utilities and Fairhope Sewage Treatment Plants; and The Wharf.

"We feel very fortunate to live here and be a part of the planned development and design of Baldwin County's infrastructure," says Steve Commander vice president and manager of Volkert's Foley office.

Head Companies is a diversified real estate development and holding company based in Point Clear, Alabama with additional offices located in Orange Beach, Alabama and Panama City Beach, Florida. Led by David Head and David Head, Jr., Head Companies engages in the development of residential, commercial, mixed-use and planned-unit projects throughout the northern gulf coast. Prior to developing coastal planned unit developments and resort communities, Head Companies developed multiple projects in Alabama, Florida, Georgia, Louisiana, Mississippi, Tennessee, and North Carolina, which included shopping centers, apartments and office buildings.

Spanning four decades, Head Companies is a recognized leader in the development industry and has built a reputation of producing a quality product that continues to set market trends.

Among Head Companies' most notable developments, The Beach Club (Gulf Shores, Alabama) features the amenities of a world-class destination. With its current and future planning, The Beach Club offers 165 total acres with 1,955 feet of beach frontage along the Gulf of Mexico. When complete, there will be 1,129 beachfront condominiums and 97 single-family and cottage home lots, making this project the largest destination resort in coastal Alabama.

Other benchmark developments for Head Companies include multi-award winning Wild Heron and the Greg Norman-designed Shark's Tooth Golf Club (Panama City, Florida) and Laterra (St. Augustine, Florida) located within premier World Golf Village neighborhood, the King & Bear, also features a world-class spa, the first ever to bear the PGA TOUR® designation. In addition to Wild Heron, other highly

recognized residential golf communities developed by Head Companies include Peninsula (Gulf Shores, Alabama), Rock Creek (Fairhope, Alabama), and Marcus Pointe (Pensacola, Florida). Indigo (Perdido Key, Florida), most recently completed by Head Companies in late 2005, set record sales in the area when the first Phase sold within only four hours plus a waiting list for the additional units offered in Phase II.

In testament to Head Companies' commitment to excellence, their projects continue to be recognized by planners and builders for the impressive quality of their design and construction.

For more information about Head Companies' developments, please visit their website at www.headcompanies.com.

❖

Above: Indigo, Perdido Key, Florida.

Bottom, right: The Beach Club, Gulf Shores, Alabama.

Bottom, left: Wild Heron, Panama City, Florida.

MERCY MEDICAL

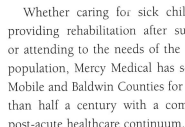

Whether caring for sick children, providing rehabilitation after surgery or attending to the needs of the aging population, Mercy Medical has served Mobile and Baldwin Counties for more than half a century with a complete post-acute healthcare continuum.

First established by the Sisters of Mercy, Baltimore Regional Community in 1949 as Villa Mercy in Daphne, Mercy Medical began as a convalescent home with the mission of continuing the healing ministry of Jesus by providing excellent and compassionate holistic healthcare. Through their healing spirit and sense of social responsibility, the Sisters of Mercy have had a significant impact on the lives of people in South Alabama.

In 1964 the organization opened a fifty-four-bed nursing home. Eleven years later, Mercy changed its emphasis to rehabilitation and therapy services. Inpatient hospice services were first established in 1979 and, in 1981, home health services began in Baldwin and Mobile Counties. The organization changed its name in 1987 to Mercy Medical and also began its endeavor into assisted living.

A year later, Mercy Medical received licensure as an acute rehabilitation hospital with twenty-five-beds. In the early 1990s, the Daphne rehabilitation hospital was built to include skilled nursing and therapy services. The company also opened Mercy Medical-Mobile, a twenty-bed skilled nursing and hospice unit on Dauphin Street.

In 1993, Mercy Medical opened McAuley Place assisted living and Portier Place lifecare communities. In response to a growing need, the Pediatric Home Care program began in 1998 offering full-range, home healthcare services to pediatric patients.

The Hamlet is a lifecare retirement community, which opened in 2001 with nine cottages and a clubhouse in Fairhope. Then in 2002, The Hamlet opened nine additional cottages, Carroll Place assisted living community expanded and Catherine Place assisted living opened in Daphne.

For Mercy Medical, 2004 was a landmark year. The organization named Mary Kay Polys as its new president and chief executive officer following Sister Mary Eileen Wilhelm's thirty-seven-year tenure as Mercy's chief administrator. Mercy also opened the $3.6 million John McClure Snook Regional Center, the region's only state licensed and certified specialty care assisted living center for Alzheimer's and other dementias.

One of the area's largest employers, Mercy Medical's more than 600 employees provide healthcare to people of all ages, working from ten different locations in both Mobile and Baldwin Counties.

Today, the organization's integrated network of services includes rehabilitation, skilled nursing, home health, long-term care, Alzheimer's care, assisted living and lifecare communities, and hospice. The Joint Commission on Accreditation of Healthcare Organizations accredits Mercy Medical.

Mercy Medical provides individuals the opportunity for enhanced quality of life through the integration of medical management, rehabilitative services, wellness and residential communities. Mercy's care is characterized by a courageous and creative response to the needs of its patients and residents.

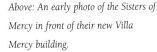

❖

Above: An early photo of the Sisters of Mercy in front of their new Villa Mercy building.

Below: The current Wilhelm Administration building on the Mercy Medical campus in Daphne.

Lartigue Fresh Seafood Market is a family owned and operated business that specializes in locally caught seafood from the Gulf of Mexico. The business was founded by Paul Jr. and Larry Lartigue, who opened their first seafood market at 4503 Old Shell Road in Mobile, Alabama also known as Spring Hill in 1979.

Three years later Paul bought his brother's half of the business. Larry opened another seafood business on Moffett Road in Mobile, which he sold after about four years to become a charter boat captain.

Paul Lartigue III attended Clark College in Newton, Mississippi on a baseball scholarship in 1986, and his brother Roger tended t he family business. Realizing that he was needed to work in the business, Paul III left college and committed to the family business as a career.

In 1988, Paul Jr. bought Gulf Stream Seafood in Mobile, relocated it to Gulf Shores as Lartigue Fresh Seafood Market Inc., with the Old Shell Road location being Lartigue Seafood Inc. They remodeled a duplex condominium they purchased in Gulf Shores, with a small seafood market in front and a private residence in back. Paul III and Roger operated the business in Mobile for eight years.

When the elder Lartigues decided to retire in 1997, Roger took charge of the Mobile store and Paul III of the Gulf Shores location. Although the businesses are separate, the brothers utilize their joint purchasing power to buy the freshest shrimp, crab meat and fish on the Gulf Coast from seafood suppliers in Louisiana, Mississippi, Florida and Alabama.

In addition to selling seafood, they now create many seafood specialty items, including stuffed crabs, fish, shrimp, shrimp Creole, seafood gumbo and more, from their USDA Board of Health-approved kitchen.

Having outgrown the Gulf Shores location, they relocated it to a larger facility they built on a commercial lot on Highway 182 in Orange Beach, Alabama. They invite everyone to come by and visit and experience the real deal in fresh and steamed seafood to go.

"Cooking Since 1979 and Still Cooking."

LARTIGUE FRESH SEAFOOD MARKET

PIER 33, INC.

❖

Pier 33.

Regarded as Alabama's southernmost general store and Gulf Shores' oldest grocery store, Pier 33 has it all—from groceries and beach apparel to fishing tackle, souvenirs and beach toys.

Tom Cook founded the landmark in 1978 at the urging and support of his father, Harvey, who was in the wholesale grocery business and wanted to give his son a good start in the business as well. The perfect property was located at 900 West Beach Boulevard, and was purchased on Tom's thirty-third birthday. That meant the perfect name for the beach store would be Pier 33.

When it was opened to customers in 1978, Pier 33 was one of only two or three grocery stores in the area, and today the only one still in business. The success of the store and its many devoted employees and customers was tested in 1979 when Hurricane Frederick wreaked havoc upon the area and destroyed the fledgling business. Only a year later, Pier 33 was rebuilt and opened to its grateful customers.

In 2004, Hurricane Ivan made a direct hit on Gulf Shores. The Pier 33 building survived but had extensive damage and was closed for six months while repairs were made. Gulf Shores' oldest grocery store was "new" again.

The Pier 33 staff has contributed greatly to the success of the business with five employees having been with the company for seventeen to twenty-six years.

As the store is approaching its thirtieth anniversary, Pier 33 continues to offer a wide range of items to the third generation of Gulf Shores residents and visitors.

ORIGINAL OYSTER HOUSE AND BAYOU VILLAGE

The Original Oyster House Restaurant is the result of two dedicated families. Joe and Mary Lou Roszkowski and David and Jane Dekle started their successful local seafood restaurants in 1982. Joe was executive chef at the Gulf State Park in Gulf Shores, Alabama when he met his soon to be business partner, David. David worked for a local distribution company, Fruit Distributing when he made a sales call to Joe at the State Park this begun their business relationship and the start of their partnership. Joe is president of the Original Oyster House, David is vice president and Mary Lou Roszkowski is the director of operations.

In May 1983, the Original Oyster House opened its doors in the Bayou Village Shopping Center in Gulf Shores with sixty seats and ten employees. After two expansions in 1986 and 1996, it now seats 250 and employs 110 people. Not only is it the oldest seafood restaurant on Pleasure Island it is nestled in Bayou Village, the area's oldest specialty shopping center, which they purchased in 1996. They also purchased an additional lot in 2004 for needed parking.

With the success of the first restaurant, a second was opened on the Causeway in Mobile, Alabama in 1985 with eighty seats. It too was expanded numerous times over the years to eventually include a gift shop, boat dock and additional 280 seats.

Over the years, hurricanes, especially George, Ivan and Katrina have played a part in the history of all three businesses. Causing irreparable damage to the Mobile Causeway restaurant in 2005, Hurricane Katrina was responsible for the restaurant's move to a new building, two miles east on the Causeway. Hurricane Ivan closed the Gulf Shores restaurant and shopping center for five weeks.

The Original Oyster House continues to support the community by involvement in charitable organizations as well as donating to area schools and churches. In addition, we support the Alzheimer Foundation, American Red Cross and Child Advocacy. We also sponsor the Alabama Gulf Coast Annual National Shrimp Festival, Delta Blues Festival, Annual Alabama Coastal Cleanup, Chelsea Garvin Spirit Award Scholarship and the Annual Priest Appreciation Dinner to name just a few.

Over their twenty-five years in business together, Joe and Mary Lou Roszkowski and David and Jane Dekle have always strived to meet their mission statement, "Exceeding our customers' expectations with the Best Employees in the World."

❖

Above: First restaurant the Original Oyster House opened in 1983 in Gulf Shores, Alabama.

Below: New location of Mobile Causeway restaurant.

VISION BANK

Vision Bank has experienced phenomenal growth since its inception in 2000. It all began with the "vision" of our Chairman and CEO, Danny Sizemore. After enjoying many years in the banking industry and with previous successful start-up banking ventures to his credit, Sizemore recognized the Alabama Gulf Coast as yet another thriving area that would benefit from a locally owned, full service and relationship oriented community bank. The Gulf Shores and Orange Beach communities were ready and waiting for the banking environment that Vision Bank planned to offer.

Sizemore visited with local residents, business owners and community leaders, and proceeded to form an alliance with a core group of investors. Vision Bancshares was organized in July 1999 to serve as the parent company for Vision Bank, an Alabama banking corporation. After raising eight million dollars in capital and receiving all regulatory approvals, Vision Bank began serving the Alabama Gulf Coast community on March 29, 2000 with twelve employees and locations in Gulf Shores and Orange Beach. Vision Bank, since its inception, has added five additional offices to its Alabama family, including locations in Foley, Elberta, Pt. Clear, Fairhope, and Daphne. The Alabama bank currently employees 100 of the best in the business.

The Company took the same vision to the panhandle of Florida in mid 2002. After raising seven and a half million dollars in capital and receiving the necessary regulatory approvals, Vision Bank, FSB, a Florida based federal savings bank organized under the Office of Thrift Supervision. It began serving the Bay County area on January 21, 2003 with locations in Panama City and Panama City Beach, Florida.

On October 15, 2004, Vision Bancshares, Inc. completed its acquisition of BankTrust of Florida located in Wewahitchka, Gulf County, Florida and changed the name of BankTrust of Florida to "Vision Bank." Subsequent to the acquisition, the Company merged Vision Bank, FSB, its wholly owned federal savings bank, with and into Vision Florida. This merger between BankTrust of Florida and Vision Bank added three Gulf County locations, Wewahitchka, Port St. Joe, and Port St. Joe Beach. In February 2005, Vision Bank opened two additional branches; Beckrich Road in Panama City Beach, and Santa Rosa Beach in Walton County. Our newest location, in Destin opened in February 2006. The Florida panhandle locations employ an impressive seventy-eight as of February 2006.

❖

Above: Danny Sizemore.

Below: Vision Bank, Foley Branch.

With a motto of "Your Hometown Advantage," United Bank proudly serves markets with hometown flare.

This is not the typical attitude of most banks, and in some cases, United Bank is not located in a typical bank building. The Silverhill Branch, for example, is located in the more than 100-year-old People's Exchange building. Customers there conduct banking transactions with personal bankers at desks rather than a teller row. This friendly and inviting environment is just one element that creates a unique banking experience.

In keeping with its mission statement, "Strength Through Service Excellence," United Bank provides full services, ranging from checking and savings accounts, loans, certificates of deposit, and business accounts to Insurance Services, Investment Services, Mortgage Services and Agri-Finance Services.

The Bank of Atmore in Escambia County, Alabama, which received its charter as a state bank on January 4, 1904, was transformed into a holding company in December 1982. The transition not only merged Peoples Bank in neighboring Monroe County, it also changed its name to United Bank. The Bank of Atmore received the fifty-eighth certificate of participation from the FDIC—this low number

testifying to the bank's early beginning. The certificate number has survived two world wars, a national depression, a bank merger of its own, and still stands as the fifty-eighth member of FDIC.

In an aggressive branching program in 1996, United Bank considered Baldwin County's growing market and close proximity to the home office in Atmore vital to its expansion, opening the first branch in Baldwin County in Foley, with others following in Lillian, Silverhill, Magnolia Springs, Summerdale and a pair in Bay Minette.

Robert R. Jones III, president and CEO of United Bank, joined during the time of the expansion into Baldwin County, and still serves in that capacity.

A $385 million financial institution that has enjoyed 100 years of services, United Bank has offices in Atmore, Flomaton, Monroeville, Frisco City, Bay Minette, Silverhill, Summerdale, Foley, Magnolia Springs and Lillian, Alabama, and now serves Santa Rosa County, Florida, in both Jay and Milton. In an age of large bank mergers, United Bank plans to continue serving those searching for personal service and local decisions.

For more information, please visit the bank's website at www.ubankal.com or www.ubankfl.com.

Silverhill Branch is located in the People's Exchange building, which dates back more than one hundred years.

THE PICTURE MAN

The Picture Man has provided professional family beach portraits and wedding photography in the Baldwin County area since 1987.

Chuck and Noreen Bell opened the business when they came here from Dallas, where they had been in photography since 1972. They were drawn to Baldwin County because of their love

for the area. Chuck's mom was raised here and he had many happy vacation memories. They opened their small studio at Pelican's Landing and, after finding that most of their portraiture was done on location, began working from their home.

"We have photographed families and weddings at some of the most beautiful beaches and historic locales in Baldwin County," Chuck said. "We're a Mom and Pop organization that has grown to love this area more with each assignment."

Members of the Alabama Gulf Coast Area Chamber of Commerce and Professional Photographers of America, they often donate portraits for local fundraisers.

For more information call 251-948-3686 or visit the website that their daughter, Heather, developed and maintains for them at www.gulfshoresphotographer.com.

DELATORRE DAY SPA

Fairhope's first massage therapist, Linda Porter Delatorre, was introduced to the benefits of a relaxing massage during a stressful period when she was traveling throughout the United States and often abroad as a representative for resort developers.

Although she enjoyed traveling and thrived in the high-pressure world of handling complaints, checking punch lists and working with contractors

✧

Linda Delatorre.

and rental management companies, she often found it necessary to relax with a massage.

Dreaming of owning her own business, she trained to become a Licensed Massage Therapist (LMT) and opened her first day spa in 1986, long before day spas had been heard of in Fairhope. Although she was ahead of her time, she received support from local businesses,

including Marriott's Grand Hotel in Point Clear, which provided transportation so its guests could enjoy an hour or more of total pampering at her spa.

She subsequently accepted a number of glamorous offers to expand her horizons. She became the LMT for a number of celebrities and film companies; was the in-house LMT for New Orleans' Hotel InterContinental and the number one country club in the southeast located in Atlanta's Buckhead community; and taught her famous "Delatorre Technique," now trademarked and soon to be available online through her website, www.delaspa.com.

Wanderlust satisfied, she returned to Fairhope to be near her aging parents, Marjorie and Steven Thames, and resumed her business, which continues to grow daily as the best and most unique Day Spa in Fairhope.

SPONSORS

ABOUT THE AUTHOR

DR. LARRY BURNETTE

Dr. Larry Burnette of Lillian, Alabama, has been teaching history professionally since 1948. Dr. Burnette received his Ph.D. in history and political science from the University of Virginia. He has taught at the high school level and on the collegiate level at Birmingham Southern, Stratford College and Virginia Military Institute. He has worked as an editor for a book publisher and also as a consultant for community development. He is the author of numerous articles and monographs and has recently completed a comprehensive history of Baldwin County, titled *Coastal Kingdom: A History of Baldwin County*. Burnette is currently writing a book on the history of the Constitution of the United States.Baldwin Animal Rescue Center.

ABOUT THE COVER

BLANCHE SUMRALL

Blanche Sumrall is an Alabama artist who is well-known for her watercolors. In 1975, Sumrall began studying at the Eastern Shore Art Center. Since then, while painting in her Spanish Fort studio, she has, on occasion, taken private lessons from artists she admires. She enjoys painting flowers and fruits, seascapes, birds and other subjects.